# THE NEW IMMORALITY

*Books by David A. Redding:*

THE PARABLES HE TOLD
PSALMS OF DAVID
THE MIRACLES OF CHRIST
IF I COULD PRAY AGAIN
THE NEW IMMORALITY

# THE
# NEW
# IMMORALITY

David A. Redding

FLEMING H. REVELL COMPANY
WESTWOOD NEW JERSEY

Scripture quotations marked RSV are from the *Revised Standard Version of the Bible*, Copyright 1946 and 1952.

"A Nation Needs a Galahad" originally appeared as an article entitled "God Make Us Great," written by the author, and published in *Christianity Today*, June 22, 1962.

"Male and Female Created He Them" originally appeared as an article written by the author, and published in *Christian Herald*, October, 1964.

"Good Deeds Not to Do" originally appeared as an article written by the author, and published in *Christian Herald*, October, 1965.

In Chapter 7, the lines from *Murder in the Cathedral*, by T. S. Eliot, are reprinted with the permission of the publishers, Harcourt, Brace & World, Inc.

Scripture passages marked KJV are from the *King James Version of the Bible*.

# ACKNOWLEDGMENTS

*Sandra Jo Cook*
*Berta Lebock Nock*
*Louise Allen Peters*
*Dorothy McCleery Redding*
*John Maxwell McCleery, M.D.*

# PREFACE

How do you tell the difference between right and wrong? Should you tattle on your roommate if some honor system demands it? Can the court compel you to tell the whole truth even if it means betraying a confidence? Are there ever any special occasions when God throws His commandments in reverse: *Thou shalt steal*—a dime to make an emergency phone call; *thou shalt kill*—to defend your child; *thou shalt commit adultery*—if, as Joseph Fletcher suggests in *Situational Ethics*, having a child were the only way a woman could be freed from a Soviet prison camp?

By what rule of thumb, then, do you read the commandments to your son to squire him safely through the squeeze-play of modern moral decisions? How do you plan to pick your own way through the haze that sophisticated temptation casts over plain old black and white? Some Christian judges in Hitler's Germany bravely refused resignation, calling it a coward's way of deserting their cases to cruel hands; others bravely refused to salute an obnoxious swastika. Who did right?

The burning issue before us is that the beloved old map of the moral world, handed down so faithfully in our Christian family, is in danger of being pulled to pieces. The revered tablets which have long ruled the conscience of the West, unquestioned, are now being rudely bombarded by the novel ambiguities of what existentialists are announcing is "a world come of age." Moses may have spoken for God once and for all: "Thou shalt. . . ." Jean Paul Sartre could not care less; he fires his broadsides from a nowhere of antinomian relativity, improvising off-the-cuff morals to suit the "God is dead" hypothesis.

You and I cannot afford to take this controversy sitting down, for our future depends on what we intend to do about it. Moses cried: "Lay to heart all the words which I enjoin upon you this day, that you may command them to your children, that they may be careful to do all the words of this law. For it is no trifle for you, but it is your life . . ." (DEUTERONOMY 32:46-7, RSV). We must not be afraid to ask if the current moral cutups are truly *honest to God;* nor should we be afraid to investigate whether God was completely *honest to man* before our generation got involved in this question. How timely are these timeless absolutes? Is God's Sinai correspondence still in force in Times Square tonight? Do we need Deuteronomy any more, now that we have the North American Headquarters Air Defense Command neatly tucked away under Cheyenne Mountain?

The caveman felt "all's fair in love and war." However, doing what comes naturally didn't wear so well with his impulsive friends and relatives; so when spontaneous cavemen began rooming together, certain ground rules were grudgingly acknowledged to keep them from getting blood all over each other all the time. Thus, the first stabs at society thrust everybody headlong into moral issues; and each culture thereafter was called to order upon approved conduct and fell apart with its collapse. *Babylon* is still a bad word for a culture that distinguished its extinction by its immorality.

And then, as Albert Schweitzer has observed, "Between the eighth and sixth centuries B.C., thinking men belonging to three nations, living in widely separated countries and having no relations whatever with one another, rise one and all to the perception that the ethical consists not in submission to traditional national customs, but in the active devotion of individuals to their fellowmen or to aims which should produce an improvement of social conditions. . . . The Jewish prophets, Amos and Isaiah (760–700 B.C.), Zarathustra (7th century B.C.) and Kungtze (560–480 B.C.), mark the great turning points in the spiritual history of mankind" (Albert Schweitzer, *Out of My Life and Thought*). This development finally burned at its brightest in what Christians revere as *The Great Commandment*.

The systematic study of ethics first flourished among the Greeks, who furnished the word *ethos*, meaning "character." They took the subject to mean the evaluation of what a man, or men, ought to do. If the Babylonians at their worst remind us of the extremities of passion, the Greeks at their best make us think of pure reason. Socrates started us off, according to Plato, saying that being good was simply a matter of education, and immorality merely ignorance.

The Judaeo-Christian tradition contradicted the wisdom of Athens with Paul's words: "For the good that I would I do not: but the evil which I would not, that I do" (ROMANS 7:19, KJV). Yet that matchmaker, Aquinas, managed to marry Aristotle's reasoning with the revelation of Israel, rocking Hellenic armchair philosophy with action. One God gave the Greek pantheon a piece of *His* mind—it was not idle talk, but Good News, giving birth to deeds of mercy.

The study of modern ethics stretches philosophically from Augustine to Bonhoeffer, from medievalists, such as Duns Scotus, to demythologizers-come-lately, such as Rudolf Bultmann, not to mention an agnostic sage from the

Orient named Confucius and a contemporary humanist named Walter Lippmann, whose *Preface to Morals* has recently been reprinted.

The three fathers of our philosophy of Western ethics are Kant, Hegel, and Schleiermacher. They form the departure point for the current debate. The moral to Kant was motive and will: life cries out to you a categorical imperative—or else! Hegel developed the equation: thesis versus antithesis equals synthesis (and this mentality mothered Marx: proletariat versus capitalist equals the classless society). Morality got emotional under Schleiermacher, which aroused Sören Kierkegaard's deeply Christian existentialism; yet this finally set off a reckless chain-reaction until morality has become nothing more than "loving conflict" to such innovators as Marcel. Nietzsche reacted violently against the entire tradition of Christian ethics. He tried to shove Darwin to a logical moral conclusion, condemning peace-loving Christian qualities as "slave virtues." Nietzsche reveled in the "brute strength" of a Napoleon; so did Hitler.

Shall you and I specialize in one major ethic? Grotius exalted the keeping of promises. Schweitzer, in his *Philosophy and Ethics*, celebrated the slogan: "Reverence for Life." The Epicureans appreciated the highest pleasure; the Navahos cherished the greatest courage. To be different, you and I can become Logical Positivists or Utilitarians.

Jiminy Cricket kept Pinnochio's conscience. To whom shall we go to credit or to complain when our conscience acts up? As Huck Finn said, "Sometimes a feller's conscience takes up more room than all the rest of a person's insides."

Everyone knows that something ails the legalist. This display-window man who keeps the rules letter-perfect at the expense of the right spirit is making a grave mistake. Keeping the commandments is a quick hop to hell if one is proud of it and negative about it. The church is tortured, as the synagogue used to be, by these impersonal and unpleasant Puritans heartlessly ramming down their ironclad *do's* and *don'ts.*

Morals frozen in general must be thawed and served in particular by warmer spirits, such as St. Francis of Assisi who lived up to Augustine's maxim: "Love Christ and do as you please." The new life rightly dreads the dry, mechanical importation of legislation from yesterday. After all, as Einstein perceived, here we are moving through space in seven different directions at once; even the star from which the navigator is taking his fix, may have burned out forty light years before. The law of gravity is always true, but it can be overruled. So, in a sense, it is relative to the situation, and one can easily see how rapidly the eternal verities can be complicated by subjective rationalization. Since love is uppermost, and "never ends," how far does it go, and exactly where, in a given instance? We cannot know finally, until that time.

Stretching morals to suit this plastic predicament is what is meant by the New Morality, and that brings us immediately to its problem. Telling a susceptible teen-ager, headed for the back seat of a car, to "love the meaningful" may not be sufficiently explicit to meet the practical pressures of her temptation. In advance, she must know when and where she is going to say "no," or be at the mercy of subjective emotion that may scar her permanently. Without the strategy of being guided in advance by commandments, conscience itself is footloose in the heat of battle. The pressures of the moment will overpower us unless we have prior commitments. Beyond this, without mutually accepted standards of conduct, we have no way of protecting each other from our own moral anarchy. For instance, a Beatnik might establish what some would call "a meaningful rela-

· 13 ·

tionship" with a girl, but to her father it would still be rape. Ethics need to learn how to use a dictionary. A morality that scorns boundary lines is "loose living." Let us have no horror of definitions. "Good fences make good neighbors." Our quarrel, as Kale Kline makes clear, is not with the moral but the moralistic; we object to being legalistic but not to being legal.

Howard Lowry, in an address, "The Fifth Year," abhors the anarchy that comes when "every man becomes a law unto himself." Without some criteria spelled out, how can one know whether he is hearing voices or "the still small voice"? Unless a man has some specific references outside his own field of influence, he faces the sleazy relativism satirized "by the comment of a famous writer that we should not be too hard on one of his contemporaries who only lies when he is very tired" (*The Wooster Alumni Bulletin*, July, 1965). It is healthy, too, to have this distinguished college president recall that remarkable six-hundred-year-old prayer of Jacopone Da Todi: "O Thou who lovest me, set this love in order." So that love would not be a spineless lump, God gave love character and faced it in with commandments. Addison H. Leitch, author of the timely *Winds of Doctrine*, finds Calvin saying, in effect: "Without the spirit the law is dead. Without the law the spirit is frantic." God *rules* creation, disciplining His love; specifying liberty, not license.

Only God Himself knows the difference between right and wrong in each unique instance, and so the ultimate solution in every human situation is for us to pray. One can memorize all the laws and the prophets, and maintain the most saintly conscience, but that will not be sufficient to discern what is right for him just then. Every man who wants to do right is forced, finally, to go beyond both anarchy and government to wait upon God for a very special, and deeply personal reply. Elisabeth Elliot has helped to make this finer distinction by reminding us that Jesus did not say: "*This* is the way," or "*This* is the truth," but rather, "*I* am the way, the truth, and the life . . ." (JOHN 14:6, KJV).

Finding the will of God, in detail, for you today has to wait on your initial decision to *do* the will of God with your whole life everyday. Even after that huge adjustment, how does one ever know whether it is God's will he follows, or only what he wants? Such a pilgrimage is schooled in trial and error; the quest always escapes us, but for the grace of God.

The succeeding chapters take up the familiar moral battlefields in which each of us must make his stand and hold fast the faith. We will need persistence. We will need friends. We will learn humility the hard way. Time after time, we will be up against a wall where either to resist or to surrender seems impossible. The tempter never let Christ alone, even on the cross.

O Earth, your name is Gethsemane! Yet when our hope and strength are gone, out of the heartbreak and the darkness will open unexpectedly a shining path larger than either of these; instead of two men everlastingly locking horns, or one man cornered, cowering, deathly sick in his sin, the climate changes, charged by a reigning, interposing Presence. As a blessed Christian gently reminded me, we shall find our way near the jagged point of our despair, as the desolate Marys found that morning, as they approached the tomb: the huge stone had already been rolled away.

*David A. Redding*

# CONTENTS

# I

# THE DECISION

# 1

# A Nation Needs a Galahad

BACK IN THE old days of China, an emperor built a gigantic wall to defend the country against the barbarians to the north. It stretched for miles along the border, and it was wide enough for chariots to pass on top. It remains one of the wonders of the world, perhaps the one man-made object that will be visible from the moon. But as a defense effort the wall was a dud. The enemy breached it by merely bribing a gatekeeper.

We fork over almost all that's in our national pocket now to be policed around the clock. It would be suicide not to take these precautions, but it is foolhardy for us to think that they are adequate. Communist screams distract us from our moral health and Christian obligations. It would be heart-breaking, after all the bankrupting military effort we have spent, if the bottom fell out of the integrity of the American people and our monumental Dew Line became our gravestone—just as the Great Wall marks the tomb of the Chinese Empire.

We are not imagining things when we express anxiety over the moral condition of America. The soldiers whose brains were washed in Korea were symptoms. It made us sick to see the way communes swallowed up homes in Red China; yet some kind of monster is gulping them down in our country. More than a half million homes will be

· 21 ·

consumed this year. What will happen to the children? Former Harvard President James B. Conant warns of the smoldering social dynamite in the slums: the dark-skinned teen-ager out of school, out of work. No one wants him, not even mother. The shady sides of our cities are crawling with these young criminals, and it is not even safe in our nation's capital after dark. There are more female barmaids (not counting barflies) today. What kind of mothers will they make? The campus is not unsullied; some of the most impressive classrooms and field houses harbor cheating. At night, a golf course can be a brothel. Even the Communists are complaining about the moral listlessness of our movies. But think of so many Americans, fixed night after night to the almost vacant stare of TV! And if the average American can no longer trust his marriage partner to keep the most sacred vow over two times out of three, how soon shall we post a dishonest gatekeeper at the wrong place?

An adolescent republic, grown prodigal, should run back to its founding fathers for more faith and light. Why did we ever leave "the old country" in the first place? What did our fathers die for? What heritage is ours "to have and to hold" that some of our young political colleagues at the United Nations don't know about? What makes a nation great?

Thomas Jefferson's words call us back to our good upbringing: "I have sworn upon the altar of God eternal hostility against every form of tyranny over the mind of man." How can we take that negatively? Those words declare war against communism, any Ku Klux Klan or inquisition, too-heavy industry, too-loud labor, too much government, the chain of sin, the bonds of unbelief.

But liberty was not our fathers' first love. Freedom is the fruit of the Christian faith. Was Jefferson a Christian? He said he was. And he was not afraid to admit, "The God who gave us life gave us liberty." Liberty is not to be taken lightly simply as our inalienable right; it is a sacred trust for which we must answer to God Himself. We pledge our allegiance "under God." We are free only if we are subject to Him. Our land will be bright with "freedom's holy light" only so long as we can pray fervently, "Protect us by Thy might, great God our King." Jefferson's voice cracks like a whiplash across the face of sacrilege: "Can the liberties of a nation be secure when we have removed a conviction that these liberties are the gift of God? Indeed I tremble for my country when I reflect that God is just, that His justice cannot sleep forever" (The Jefferson Memorial, Washington, D.C.). There is only one place where liberty can possibly be: ". . . where the Spirit of the Lord is, there is liberty" (II CORINTHIANS 3:17, KJV). All else is license.

Paul's words alarm us to our Christian battle stations. Liberty is a way of saving our opportunity to serve God.

If, once more, we could see our country not on our own, or at the whim of communism, but as the servant of God, creation might stop shaking and begin to make some sense again. The chaos of our national philosophy would become clear. We would rediscover our place, our importance to God; we would recover the precious relief of security. The shrieks of bullies would dissolve in that perspective. Panic would be inconceivable among a people who knew *firsthand* that they could trust their King.

The editors of *Christian Herald* embraced a quaking year with words worthy of our heritage: "The future is as dark as the threats of men. Or the future is as bright as the promises of God. . . . Does Lenin tower above Christ? Do we say, 'This one, God, is too tough for You—we'll handle it ourselves'?" Perhaps our trouble today is that men fear

· 23 ·

men rather than God. Christianity could put our picture right side up and restore to God responsibility which only His shoulders are broad enough to bear.

Our belief begins with God, but it brings out the best in men. Ours is not a "do nothing" faith. "The Christian's strength," as the *Herald's* editors discerned, "is not in having done nothing to stand; but in having done all to stand." To believe means to obey—to go back to church imaginatively, to get under the covers of the Book afresh. We will have to restore relevantly the ways as well as the walls of Williamsburg. Today's extremity is our tutor—to teach us that carrying a nuclear knife is not enough to keep our nation safe. Tennyson's Galahad said:

> My strength is as the strength of ten,
> Because my heart is pure.

We could use a Galahad at every gate. For we have to be ready any minute now, not only to fight, but to outlive, outlove, outlast the foe, to win the right to say, "Such as we were, we gave ourselves outright" (Robert Frost).

If we can look up from checking our ammunition long enough to practice up on this old faith, we can get through this crisis as our fathers got through theirs. If we actually depend upon God, we can depend upon each other to put up a Christian fight. Fear will freeze us to death; but faith will find the practical way. Then, when we look back upon these "sixties," we too shall be able to say what George Mason said about our newborn country after the "seventies" were safely over almost two centuries ago: "It seemed as though we had been treading on enchanted ground."

# 2

# Brotherhood or Else

BROTHERHOOD USED TO be a bright idea. Now, with the threat of the bomb throbbing in our heads, our motto sobs, "Brotherhood or Else." Questions that have been haunting man since Adam's anguish over Cain and Abel are now screaming for solution. Today it would be suicide for Cain to kill Abel.

While we are busy digging our tunnels of Babel into the ground for shelter from the blast, we had better be thinking of something superior, something that will work, for not even the late General Douglas MacArthur thought that self-defense would win the peace. No one believes we can permit Ivan or Chou to bully us, but we had better believe more than that if we are ever to hang on together on this cosmic firecracker. Rigging bigger burglar alarms for SAC's warning system, breeding lethal hound-dogs by the hundreds, won't melt the hearts of men. Present tactics aren't even preparing us for the war that some clairvoyant sees: Russia and the West fighting together against China. God forbid! Whatever happens, the military doesn't make as much sense any more, now that our own side is in almost as much danger from our warheads as the enemy. All of us, friend and foe alike, are stuck in the same boat, each armed to the teeth with weapons as deadly to those behind the barrel as in front: "The world is now too dangerous for anything . . . but brotherhood" (E. Powell Davies, *Ethical Outlook*).

In World War II, one of the bravest soldiers I knew had his entire platoon wiped out twice, except for him and several wounded. He came home, his chest draped with decorations, vowing he would never fight again. He spoke not from fear, but from despair of our ever getting anywhere by war. This man has had all the war he wants. What are you and I doing to stop the next dogfight between brothers?

The Reverend Maurice McCracken, a Presbyterian minister in Cincinnati, Ohio, decided several years ago that the only way to arrest this madness mushrooming before our very eyes was to refuse to pay that portion of his income tax that went for munitions. Finally, to prick the country's attention, he refused to file an income tax at all, forcing the police to carry him in and out of court. I think he was wrong, but he was not as wrong as many think, and he certainly was no crackpot. I knew Mac as a neighbor of rare sincerity; he was determined to do *something* to prevent that fatal nuclear fit. I have often felt that his stand was far superior to one of sedated watching while the war machine is winding up for the final time.

Mr. McCracken's defense before the church court was on the grounds of "Freedom of Conscience." He was pursuing world brotherhood free of constitutional encumbrances, and his denomination's constitution guarantees that "God alone is Lord of the conscience." Civil disobedience has had a Christian tradition ever since Peter and the Apostles shocked the authorities: "We must obey God rather than men" (ACTS 5:29, RSV). The American Revolution itself originated in acts of civil defiance, such as the Boston Tea Party, until the colonies finally deserted England, shouting down John Bull's cries of treason with retorts of "no taxation without representation," and finally with an outright Declaration of Independence.

St. Paul explicitly suggests that we must be subject to rulers ". . . for the sake of conscience. For the same reason you also pay taxes, for the authorities are ministers of God . . ." (ROMANS 13:5–6, RSV). The glaring fact that Jesus incited no military revolution among mobs who were begging for it, that neither John the Baptist, nor Jesus ever advised a soldier to leave his post, and the brilliant vigor with which both John Calvin and Martin Luther defended "the powers that be" remind us of our allegiance to this "one nation under God." One gets the impression from reading the Reformers that civil magistrates—right or wrong, good or bad—are still permitted, if not appointed, by God. Consequently, almost all churches, besides their article on "freedom of conscience," quote I Peter to put teeth into patriotism: "Be subject for the Lord's sake to every human institution, whether it be to the emperor as supreme, or to governors as sent by him to punish those who do wrong and to praise those who do right. . . . Live as free men, yet without using your freedom as a pretext for evil; but live as servants of God. Honor all men. Love the brotherhood. Fear God. Honor the emperor. Servants, be submissive to your masters with all respect, not only to the kind and gentle but also to the overbearing. . . . For what credit is it, if when you do wrong and are beaten for it you take it patiently? But if when you do right and suffer for it you take it patiently, you have God's approval" (I PETER 2:13–21, RSV).

The conscientious objector may also suffer a guilty conscience because he forces his fellow citizens to do his fighting for him, while he stays behind to enjoy the blessings of liberty purchased at the price of others' blood. I know of a man who so abhorred bloodshed that he went to war only because he could not be guilty of making anybody else bear his blame. What's more, how can a man in good conscience obey the vote of the majority when he votes with it, but disobey when he is voted down? If everyone else indulged this prerogative, government would be gone. A citizen is not free to go his own way, but has at the outset pledged allegiance to a flag that cannot always put him first and still play fair to others. Old Earth will probably never again see a republic which tolerates such ample constitutional means for the minority to express its dissatisfaction. Certainly, any society depends upon a finer charity from its subjects than the desire to have things exactly as they would be if people lived alone and unorganized in a cave. Civilized men must make charitable concessions to the consciences of others, since upholding a constitution is one of the feats of brotherhood. Burning a draft card may therefore be a primitive tantrum as well as a symbol of a sensitive conscience.

However, *pacem in terras* rises above the cowardice of violence. World brotherhood will be built only by prayers that propel positive deeds, uttered by men who are not so busy passing ammunition that they cannot think of anything friendly to do. We may not be able to disarm Russia in one national fell swoop, but the same thing could be accomplished if each of us tried to disarm one Russian apiece. The power of the Peace Corps, the international exchange of students, the unsung humility of many missionaries incarnate the secret intelligence of brotherhood in the only war that will ever be worth winning. Conversations with the enemy (or the nearest relatives we can reach) must begin at our dining table. Dare we risk living in a world where the U.S. is only a shrinking 6 percent of the world population, and *not* making new friends fast?

How about brotherhood between black and white? A big brother can blight a younger or weaker one without knowing it. He can be ingratiatingly decent to him, robbing him of the right to disagree or be independent. The unspoken assumption beneath all the big brother's pleasantries is that the younger one will go along like a shadow in return for the other's protection. The older brother is probably completely unconscious of yanking away the younger boy's right to object, to be himself. The boy who was there first doesn't realize that the second one smiles agreement from fear or a feeling of inferiority, not from pure pleasure. Thoughtlessly, the older brother has never drawn the younger one out; he has superimposed his views on the weaker boy's bruised sensibilities, exploiting and suppressing his spirit.

The white man, who achieved his freedom first, has dominated the black man for years. When this happens in a family, the smaller boy usually suffers for it neurotically until his resentment is exposed and reconciled; when it happens in a race, we must admit that James Baldwin, often wrong, is right when he writes: "There's a bill due that has to be paid."

The white man would have to squeeze into the cramped quarters of the black man's shoes to appreciate what has happened to him psychologically over the years. Anyone who was the second child in the family—I mean the second one to be *noticed*—ought to understand this unfair racial situation. The privileged must ask how it would be to come into a world tailored to blue-eyed Anglo-Saxons. A Negro friend of mine insists that the Negro has the same complex as an ex-convict. As a left-hander, it is hard enough for me to bear the preferential treatment extended to right-handers, all the way from desks to the righthand side of the road. You don't have to be a left-hander very long to learn about discrimination; the only advantage is at first base. But imagine *always* coming up with the short end of

the stick, of being a perpetual standby, forever seeing someone else running away with all the honors and advantages.
What would it do to a man to be everlastingly coming off
second best in the conversation, the promotion; of being
forced to take a back seat, not only in the bus, but in every
respect; of never getting first pick of anything? It is as
though the game were rigged for the white man. No wonder the white man is smiling so indulgently, completely
unaware that the reason he's so conservative, wanting to
keep things as they are, is that he has all the blocks. The man
who has always had a head start is going to have to start
thinking how to make it up to the man who never had a
chance—or suffer another civil war along the lines of Baldwin's conclusion: "If we do not now dare everything, the
fulfillment of that prophecy recreated from the Bible in
song by a slave is upon us:

> God gave Noah the rainbow sign,
> No more water—the fire next time!"

The North has no right to point its finger at the South. As
a Negro humorist commented: "The Southerner doesn't
care how close the Negro gets, so long as he doesn't get too
high. The Northerner doesn't care how high the Negro
gets, so long as he doesn't get too close." As nasty as it often
is for the Negro below the Mason-Dixon Line to be denied
ballot box and just dignity in court, he has sometimes
enjoyed genuine affection from white men there which he
has seldom found in his urban ghetto in the North. The
South has kept him under a heavy thumb, but the most
liberal crusaders in the North characteristically keep him at
arm's length. His Northern friends generally live far from
any Negro homes, which makes him feel more like a socio-
logical phenomenon than good company. He doesn't usually

get to their dinner parties unless there's a rally, and he functions as Exhibit A.

The Civil War was a sin of two sides. One wonders, if the North had lost and had its nose rubbed in the indignities of reconstruction, what it would have done to all the progress in race relations we too easily suppose we have made. The right to enter restaurants and rest rooms is old business; toleration must make way for more extensive acceptance. Where can the North point with pride? Harlem? Chicago? Until recently a Negro could not get a mortgage in some big cities. Where can a vice president of a bank live—if he happens to be colored? Landlords in Negro sections of a city typically demand high rents from Negro tenants who have nowhere else to go. How many Negroes could claim us as close friends? I wish all of us could confess and make amends in a Christian way for that slip of one white man speaking to a Negro audience: "I may be white, but my heart is just as black as yours." While we obviously differ on what should be done, hell's going to break loose unless we go out of our way to do something about this "no Negroes land."

There are, of course, three brothers in this dilemma. Can the brother in the middle be brotherly toward both the Negro and the prejudiced one without antagonizing either? Can he, in fact, bring them together? Can we in the middle be bridges instead of fence-sitters or fanatics? Charity for *all* and malice toward *none* has never been tried. Two brothers take sides so swiftly to unite against a third; no one is brother to both; it is "odd man out" every time.

I mean no approval of peace at any price. How can anyone stand idly by and let an older brother bully a younger one? Yet the older one is no monster and needs much understanding; our job is not to be judge, nor father, but *brother*. To do nothing about paternalism adds fuel for "the bloody summer" kept simmering by Black Muslims; to do everything all at once stiffens the cold civil war of White Citizens Councils and the Ku Klux Klan.

While many of us may not take to the streets, civil rights is a moral issue and Christian men must be mixed up in it in such a way as to bring one brother in from the cold without driving the other out. What is so sweet about the spirit of brotherhood if we end up swapping brothers, with still only two left in the house? Brotherhood will not be much of a blessing in this country until all three brothers can sit down to supper together at the same time, in "the unity of the Spirit in the bond of peace" (EPHESIANS 4:3, KJV). In the meantime we must favor the underdog in such a way as to disarm and not defy his alienated twin.

What about our Negro brother? He is not only a victim. He is a responsible human being who has made long strides, not merely to keep up but often to out-distance his condescending brothers. The problem of some Negroes, however, may be that they are so engrossed with getting rights that they cannot think of anything for which to be thankful or apologetic. As Herbert Hoover mentioned on his ninetieth birthday: "Deeply as I feel the lag in certain areas which denies equal chance to our Negro population, I cannot refrain from saying that our 19 million Negroes probably own more automobiles than all the 220 million Russians and the 200 million African Negroes put together . . ." (Life, August 21, 1964). An underprivileged person can become so obsessed with the belief that the world owes him a living that he forgets to do anything about his plight, scorning any kindness or charity as hush money for yesterday's highway robbery. Yet such a fixation shrinks him into the kind of person who is hard to live with, an undependable and resentful person who hardly ever appreciates the other fellow. No one wants this to happen to the spiritual people who grew such giants of greatness as Booker T. Washington, George Washington Carver, Ralph Bunche, and Marian Anderson. As the Negro takes his rightful place beside his brothers, he will need to shoulder more responsibility for his own plight; he will have to prove his pride in his country by showing that he has some other things to stand for beside civil rights as so many are proving at the front in Vietnam.

The origin of the problem of brotherhood is at home in church and out. Christians, for all their sweet talk on the street, are at odds with each other. The church reproaches various sinners for not being friendly, when she has not made friends with herself. She preaches peace, though divided internally. Brotherhood's mostly her hot air so far, for she doesn't see that the reason her suspicious adolescents are at each other's throats is that the mother church is cut up into sharp dissenting little splinters of her former self. And how can she expect the world to make up and be friends if the followers of Jesus Christ cannot let bygones be bygones? Whether this would involve structural unity or unity of effort across denominational lines, "divided we fall." Nothing divides and conquers children like dissension among parents; and so this "beat generation" is helplessly at odds with God because their professing fathers bitterly disagreed. So long as the followers of Christ cannot sit down companionably to that sacred table, neither the hostile secular world nor the Holy Spirit will ever sit down among them. All of the intrachurch hair-splitting and smug indifference warn of religion's impotence and nurse the prodigality of the lost sheep. The return of modern man to God awaits the momentous reconciliation of Christendom.

# 3

# Male and Female Created He Them

MENTION MORALS, and most people immediately think of the demanding battle between the sexes. However, men and women are different in more ways than one, and the approach to sexual morality must be prefaced with an acknowledgment of the feminine mystique.

The handicap of being male is made painfully clear back in the nursery. Bustling little mothers already have the upper hand and last word, much to the embarrassment of the frustrated little fellows standing around sucking their thumbs. Brides in miniature are maturely playing house while Junior is mutely throwing blocks at the unfair competition. In high school, dolls run circles around guys, socially. When a boy is elected president of something, it is, as Dr. Paul Popenoe suggests, as a concession to a minority group, and he is exploited as a tongue-tied tool of frighteningly high-heeled coeds.

Women have recently invaded every traditionally masculine profession; yet they have managed to hang onto all the ancient privileges accorded "ladies first." Even if a woman has a Ph.D. or becomes president of a corporation, we still have to escort her across the street.

Mother never told us that the drastic distinction between

men and women is psychological. Women, for instance, are not known to waitresses as heavy tippers. A man will pay two dollars for a one-dollar article he wants; a woman will pay one dollar for a two-dollar article she doesn't want. Men are frank, but women, leading from weakness, can fool you every time. When she says "No," she may mean "Yes"—or vice versa. In self-defense, the weaker sex became Queen of the Diversionary Tactic. Since she was no match for man in muscle, she resorted to strategy. She learned to play a waiting game, exploiting hit-and-run warfare, avoiding head-on collisions by counter-attacks of cosmetics and smooth talk.

Physical inequality has made woman even more of a mystery to man than he grasps until he is into the second or third year of marriage. One evening he comes home from work, as usual, and his wife isn't there to greet him at the door. He looks in and shouts, "Dear, I'm home!" No answer. He knows she knows he's there, for he hears the steam iron squeaking back and forth with menacing regularity. Something tells him all is not well, but he is no match for her in this unnerving calm before the storm.

Just to make sure, he makes one more half-hearted stab at it: "What's wrong, honey?" From the other room comes a voice as flat and frozen as ice: "Nothing." He could cut the gloom with a knife. What did he do?

This is a woman's way of registering a negative vote. Big he-men will be brutally frank: "You forgot my birthday." The little woman will beat about the bush because hubby's love is no good to her if she has to remind him. How can he keep his mind on anything else if he's so mad about her? Brand-new bridegrooms may not be braced for this first breath of cold air. It's no use asking, "Why can't a woman be like a man?" She won't be—as if anyone really wishes she would. A man has his work as well as his wife; but a man means everything to a woman, and her emotional state is at the mercy of the attention he pays to her.

While there is a world of difference between a man and woman, there is one code of honor for both. There is no room in Christianity for a double standard of behavior. God divided us into male and female, but He made *one* set of Commandments. Men may disagree as to how they apply these Commandments, but there can be no doubt that dishonesty is as vicious between men and women as it is man-to-man. Christianity doesn't discriminate between the sexes any more than between races. Treason is treason wherever it rears its ugly head.

First of all, dating, as much as any other business, must be disciplined by faithfulness. It is not fair to say, "All's fair in love and war." We respect Launcelot because he was brave in war. But we look up to Galahad because he could be trusted to keep his vows not only on the field of battle but in the house and with another man's wife.

Chastity is not a "nice" word coined by Victorians, but rather the higher education men have learned by bitter and sweet experience. Morals are not supposed to make life harder, but happier. Morals come with intelligence: Galahad was not simply right, he was bright. Marriage is the way man gets the most satisfying physical, psychical, and spiritual pleasure out of life. The home is the climax of ageless centuries of struggle to find the solution to man's desires and dreams. Divorce and disloyalty are not improvements but reversions to the beastly life that we've supposedly outgrown.

Aldous Huxley said that if the recent rate of divorces continues to accelerate, "In a few years, no doubt, marriage licenses will be sold like dog licenses, good for a period of twelve months, with no law against changing dogs or keeping more than one animal at a time" (*Brave New World*).

· 37 ·

This is not to deny that a given divorce may not be a sensible idea; there are exceptions to the rule. Helmut Thielicke, in *The Ethics of Sex,* recognized the possibility of a church approving divorce and remarriage in a borderline case where "it was *not* God who joined the couple together, but rather that it was the persons themselves who wrongly, or carelessly, mistakenly or blindly, but in any case contrary to the order of creation, joined themselves together." But reducing marriage to a temporary arrangement for one mating season is surrendering the horse sense of the race and violently desecrating the New Testament of Christ. A promiscuous existence may be perfectly satisfactory for a spaniel, but stings with hell for any son of Adam. And according to statistics from the Institute of Family Relations, each succeeding marriage for divorced people has a 50 percent less chance for success.

This is a free country where any man or woman may go to the dogs if he or she so desires. But before we go, we should look at what we're losing. Our place in line is only "a little lower than the angels"; we cannot have our cake and eat it too. Any man at his best who secretly envies man at his worst has failed to read the price tag on the package. God has daringly given men and women their choice between unrestrained sexual indulgence and "Home, Sweet Home." No one can have both. "Free love" is a little misleading: it is free in exchange for all one's fineness. Night life never proves one's manhood; any tom cat is man's superior there. Manhood is much more demanding.

If a husband or wife never knows when he or she will be on his way to the next "engagement," the time they spend at home together will be soured by uneasiness. Any attempt at home life swiftly hardens into stony suspicion. Triangles and one-night stands are a setup for panic; they are the best-known breeding grounds for misunderstanding and hard feelings. In such an unstable environment, what child will ever know whom to call "father" or for how long? One boy from Beverly Hills told another: "I'll bet my father can lick your father," to which the other replied: "My father *is* your father."

The nomad is spoiled for anything but novelty. The grass he's got is never green enough. The roving eye will never see the joy that can come from holding one's gaze steady. The broken vow brings the broken home; and the broken home is a little bit of hell. Morals are mankind's blessed method of avoiding such agony.

The way we behave today will determine the happiness our children will know tomorrow. The most important question to a child is: "Mother and father, do you love me?" The close, and closely connected, second question is: "Do you love each other?"

An expert said, "The most important thing a father can do for his children is to love their mother." Nothing destroys little children like chronic dissension between parents. No matter how smooth everything else seems on the surface, if tension is seething beneath the amenities, it will disturb the children.

Any premarital activity that might shake the ship of matrimony will jeopardize the health and sanity of the next generation. No one in his right mind can ever say, "It's *my* life," as if his sins were committed at his expense alone. Just as each broken home may jar the lives of fifty people, so all our ultimate intimates will share in the consequences of any carelessness in our background. The more strongly the children sense that nothing can crack the rock of their domestic tranquility, the more self-confidence they will have, and the more confidence in God. Such a state of contentment naturally leans heavily on the trustworthiness developed by parents *prior* to their wedding day.

Being happy ever after is based on your behavior *before* marriage. Your future morals are being formulated by the height of your ideals in high school and the depths to which you sink during your higher education. A habit of polygamy prior to marriage will perpetuate itself later. It will take more than a big wedding to break up established patterns of misconduct. The husband or wife who has "been around" has not been preparing to settle down.

Mistakes are, of course, made, and the grace of God has redeemed both rakes and prostitutes. No life ever reaches a state of ruin beyond recall, but each sin assesses its penalty. Each disloyalty to one's wife or husband *before* they meet will become one more obstacle to be overcome. One's record will prove a strain or a strength tomorrow. Everything we are up to now will bolster or sap our partner's confidence. Anything we do that we have to hide will be hard to bear. Besides the burden of guilt, the guilty person will worry over when his indiscretions will be disclosed; the wronged party will wonder when they will recur.

If you are a young person, your bride or groom is alive and waiting for you somewhere this minute. He or she has the same high ideals you have for him or her. No one can tell you exactly how to behave on a date, but you could do worse than to do what you would recommend for your "one and only" in the same situation. The fellow has a way of finding and falling for the kind of girl he deserves. Put your dates in this perspective. How far should you go? How far do you want her to go with someone else? How would you feel about your father and mother going that far with someone besides each other? How far do you want your little sister to go? Is your contemplated behavior something you'd not mind confessing to her and to your own son some day?

Teen-agers do have to be different from their parents to

prove they are becoming independent, but they should choose constructive ways to rebel. Why hurt yourself simply to show mother that the apron strings are stretching? Go your parents one better. If you feel compelled to oppose them, do so on grounds other than immorality, or you and your future home will have to take the beating. If you really want to shock your folks, go into the ministry! You can be different without being destructive.

How do you know you're in love? For all Hollywood's heavy-handedness with this subject, it has not been around real love enough to know how to marry into it. Most magazine love stories are fabricated from artificial situations. The church is not out to scotch romance but to keep you from being cheated from the real thing. Christ came that you might have life, and have it more abundantly—*in this respect as in every other*. Christians believe that God knew what He was doing when He made male and female, and that His will for them is the best way to have the time of their lives. Christianity admits that he or she may be pleasing to the eye, but adds the pleasure of the brain and spirit. The pores and glands are supposed to play a part in the plan of God, but it is puerile to permit them the dominant role.

Homosexuality may be one of the unhappy results of a child maturing in a marriage without God. This tragedy may draft the boy whose mother dominates his life due to an emotionally weak or an industriously absent father. The mother, missing the daily discipline and intimate satisfaction of her spouse's masculine affections, takes refuge more and more in her relationship with her son, showering and finally smothering him with an engulfing maternalism from which he may be unable to escape, even in adolescence.

Surely the homosexual must have our understanding and help for the sick person he is, but Christians cannot condone homosexuality, neither for those suffering from it nor for

· 41 ·

society's sake. The new morality is gravely mistaken to approve such a gross manifestation of selfishness and ingrown psyche, particularly when its practice brings the sufferer only increasing grief and heartbreak and pushes the borderline youth over the brink. St. Paul condemned it in his letters to the Corinthians and the Romans, just as the Old Testament took it to be sinful and unnatural. . . . "male and female created he them" (GENESIS 1:27, KJV).

The only hope for the homosexual is in sublimating his tendancy through creative pursuits, more particularly in surrendering his infirmity completely to God. Jesus indicated that one could be a eunuch for the Kingdom, for God's sake; the homosexual too can find his happiness in this spiritual move which demands only acceptance of his limitations and commitment to the One for whom nothing is impossible.

Whatever more marriage is, it is at least friendship and is founded upon friendship's laws. In a year or two after the physical novelty has worn off, the mutual admiration society begins to take its coloring from each other's character. Even if she is still Helen of Troy and he remains the last word in women's taste, their personal relationships determine what they see in each other. There is nothing wrong with changing hairdos or growing beards, but camouflaging the ship will not make it more seaworthy.

Love is not something you fall into, but something you step up to. True love is not a crush but a charity. Love that will grow more exciting physically and personally has to be built on specific concessions and sacrifices made in the right spirit. Selfishness splits homes. Hopefully each partner will concentrate on his own faults and the other's rights. When this gets turned backwards, it does not mean that a couple were mismatched, but that neither gave an inch. Only mutual kindness can mend homes, and every home needs constant mending.

A wife confesses to a minister that she can no longer stand to have her husband touch her. Weren't they meant for each other? Of course, but the husband has not been paying attention to her. He has run out of compliments; he has forgotten that a happy home will not run on the inertia of the honeymoon. It is surprising how suddenly harmony may be restored if a man sends honest flowers to his wife and eagerly takes her out to dinner. Both become negative if they brood upon their own slights and forget the other's wishes.

Some wives would never think of going fishing at a husband's favorite vacation spot. Others have never had any choice about it. One may haul her husband off to the P.T.A. meeting, even if it kills him; his vacation will be her command performance. She will consume his time off with a compulsion of courtesies for people much less in need of them than he.

There are husbands who care so little for their wives' opinions that they couldn't tell what they would really like to do tonight if their lives depended on it—and their lives *do* depend on it! Some men have never listened to their wives long enough to find out where she went to grade school, yet no amount of evidence could convince them they are not the finest husbands in the world. Smugness smothers conjugality. A wife's hand must be won again *today*.

A marriage may suffer from what is mistakenly called "constructive" criticism. So much depends on someone being able to accentuate the positive; differences of opinion must be handled like high explosives. There are no good quarrels, and quarrels never clear the air. A fight's a fight, whether we use fists or adjectives, and word wounds are often worse than those made with clubs.

A recent study was made of accidents in a western trucking firm. It was found that the greatest number occurred early in the morning, soon after breakfast-table arguments.

We can imagine one of them beginning innocently enough. A husband probably made some crack about the coffee, and since a wife's hair was up and her blood sugar low, it sounded like fighting words. She couldn't resist throwing in something about his mother, and that did it! It went from scandal to libel until he was tearing out of the driveway, unable to see the road, spinning gravel on his way to collision.

Never quarrel at breakfast; nor when he comes home from work; nor after lights out. *Never quarrel*. If differences of opinion have to be discussed, discuss them over dinner by candlelight.

The business of husband and wife is not to "have it out" nor to get some things straight. The big idea is to make the other person feel like royalty; the whole art of lovemaking is based upon this. The home opens her treasures only in an atmosphere of mutual trust and imaginative good will. Love takes two people trying to outdo each other in the first good word for the other in front of others. Love is the determination to look at the bright side of the most depressing hat or casserole; of clearing with each other on the overtime away from home; of standing in each other's shoes long enough to be sure when to spring the right surprise.

Obviously, such an angelic situation takes some doing on God's part. Being the first to make up is a miracle of His grace. No man nor woman can make a go of marriage at this elevation of happiness without such inspiration; magnanimity demands outside help. Two people gradually go blind staring into each other's eyes. They must look out the window together, seeking the Light by which to live, and without this common devotion to this common delight, they are undone.

# 4

# The Ten Commandments

MEN AND WOMEN come and go. The Ten Commandments came to stay; men are still being broken trying to
break them. Centuries before the Bible became a Book, the
children of Israel ticked off the Commandments in a
finger-exercise of memory. They in turn taught the whole
world.

Temporary space capsules will soon give way to transient
silent wings, but these sturdy old Commandments still seem
young, if not in vogue. Unlike most classics which seem
stuck in the mud of their native millenniums, this little list of
laws loves change, makes itself at home in any clime, leaps
from age to age, completely oblivious to the aging process
already wrinkling the current controversy over morality.

A sophomore says, "Dad, today's different from when
you were a boy." He's right—and wrong, too, for his
Adam's apple is much the same as it was way back when.
The Bible needs no updating so far as human nature goes.
Modern requirements multiply astronomically, and men try
to make them fill the gap the Ten Commandments leave. No
society can escape controls. Even a band of thieves breaks
up if thieving breaks out among them. A woman operating a
house of prostitution reported her two business principles
with pride: first, she never hired an inexperienced girl; and
second, she never accepted any engagements herself. The

most permissive scoundrel may harp on hygiene. So long as we are able to play the game of life at all, we shall have some kind of minimum standards. The question smarts: "How high shall they be?" The ten specifications that Moses proposed have a power to shame and stir us still. We cannot deny to this day that Someone has given them a certain standing.

The Ten Commandments came out of the Exodus from Egypt about three thousand years ago. While the escapees were catching their breath on the other side of the Red Sea, after that mad dash from Ramses, God invited their leader Moses to ascend Sinai.

God introduced Himself dramatically as a Saviour, not as an ethical referee. "I am the Lord your God, who brought you out of the land of Egypt, out of the house of bondage" (EXODUS 20:2, RSV). The watershed in history was that Red Sea crossing, not the drawing up of the rules. The moral legislation was simply the golden afterthought to that momentous miracle which reverberates from one end of the Old Testament to the other. The divine voice was no grim attorney's, spouting abstract jurisprudence, but "You know Me, for I am the One who saved you."

*Thou shalt have no other Gods before me* (EXODUS 20:3, KJV). The ancient world was stuffed with gods. Such gods as they were, were specialists, selected for their alleged powers of fertility or rain. Religion used to mean a civil war of gods struggling for superiority, shattering men's responsibility into such sharp little pieces that men were bewildered by their overlapping obligations. A man never knew which god to trust or which one was working for or against him. Praying panic-stricken to a horde of erratic gods was not much comfort.

The First Commandment is still in force and far beyond

us. Modern man is as susceptible to a polygot of gods as his primitive ancestors. His ego may even be more difficult to control, for man now has more sophisticated ways of avoiding one God. We may not worship the moon any more; we may even laugh at the amulets of the savage; but that does not keep our hearts from fastening pathologically onto a sports record, a dream house, or *idol*izing that wife or boy of ours. How many men worship their business so obsessively that they wither and die upon retirement from it? Tom Wolfe believes the totem of many Americans is their morning newspaper. Gods have multiplied since the time of Mesopotamia, and personalities seem to split more easily now than in the days when demons divided them.

Our world has not outgrown Moses. His "First Word" is more than appropriate for our desperation. Mankind could be melted into children of one Father by keeping his command. "No man can serve two masters . . ." (MATTHEW 6:24, KJV). Jesus saved Legion from nodding dizzily to dozens of gods and safely integrated him about One. Moses is waiting for an age riddled with golden calves to catch up to this supreme fundamental. We cannot state the necessity of this First Commandment strongly enough, the other nine shine in the glory of this one. Christ Himself reaffirmed it, elaborating upon it with another phrase He found in Leviticus to make the greatest commandment of all: ". . . love the Lord thy God with all thy heart, and with all thy soul, and with all thy mind, and with all thy strength . . ." (MARK 12:30, KJV).

*You shall not make yourself a graven image* . . . (EXODUS 20:4, RSV). The First Command declares that God is One, the second that He is Spirit. Images are distracting, so this specification preserved God from the woodcarver's knife, preventing man from copying Him in something that could be carted around and bought or sold. So when one penetrates "Into the most sacred heart of the tabernacle, to the ark of the holy of holies, one finds that it is empty" (*The Interpreter's Bible*, vol. I, p. 928)—except perhaps for an unseen Presence. Within was not a place for whittlers.

God cannot be locked in dead wood nor in cold marble. Moreover, He is not to be confused with any creed or dogma. God is in motion, surpassing all our ideas of Him. Elisabeth Elliot's novel *No Graven Image* exposes those who break this commandment by cramming Christ into a stereotyped form of Christian expression, as though every man must always meet God in the same old theological rut, and be required to report it according to a fixed pattern of expression. A dynamic faith in a personal Father evades static definition. Our athletic God refuses to assume a rigid ecclesiastical pose in a stationary shrine. He is alive and free to surprise us with unpredictable mercies. ". . . the day of the Lord will come like a thief in the night" (1 THESSALONIANS 5:2, RSV). Since God is no graven image, meeting Him and minding Him will never be repetitious; it will be an incomparable personal exchange. This rule protects us against the idle rumor that "God is dead."

*You shall not take the name of the Lord your God in vain* . . . (EXODUS 20:7, RSV). Warnings to "Keep Off the Grass" often carry more weight than this old admonition now. Among primitive peoples, a rose by any other name would *not* smell as sweet. A name to them was inseparable from that which was named. Pronouncing the name invoked that person's power, and so abuse of a divine name was criminal.

Swearing has since become a national pastime, a valve for the inarticulate. What does such carelessness signify? How would you feel if your name leaped to your neighbor's lips when he lost his temper? What must God think if, when we are searching for the worst word we can think of, His name is the first to come to mind? The fact that we curse without thinking, that this practice is so deep in us as to be almost unconscious, makes the sin worse.

How do we explain the fact that we have flung upon the bonepile the holy vocabulary our fathers would have died before adulterating? If it does not reflect blasphemy, does it not reflect a more despicable boredom, perhaps a deep-seated obstinacy against the whole idea of God and His goodness and authority over us? Freud reminded us that talk is not cheap, that no slip of the tongue was ever accidental, but terribly revealing. Jesus said we would be held responsible for every *word* we uttered. No son who cares for his father from the depths of his being will automatically mutter obscenities against him to find his self-expression. Words carry their weight in gold or God-forsakenness. Perhaps the thoughtless disgrace we bring to the holy name of God is done only with malice aforethought.

*Remember the sabbath day, to keep it holy* (EXODUS 20:8, KJV). God climaxed creation with a day of rest, according to Genesis. Somehow the idea that this belief was built in from the beginning was so impressed upon the Jews that they wrote it indelibly into the human race. The moon is made to make a change every fourteen days, and man found he had to rest in half that time.

As time went on, this sacred interval became more trouble than it was worth. Instead of bringing relief, it became an exhausting burden. Oppressive regulations accumulated across the centuries until the sabbath was a nightmare of deadlines instead of the sweetness of godly rest.

"They said" Jesus broke the sabbath, but they were wrong. Jesus broke off the growth of man-made minutiae clinging to it, and made it like new. The sabbath, He insisted, was originally made for man, and not man for the sabbath; it was to be a privilege, not a penalty. This does not mean that anything goes on the sabbath, nor that it should be indistinguishable from any other day. It is God's day for man's sake, and is not to be taken lightly. There is room for special application, but sabbath-keeping is an order Jesus Himself obeyed: ". . . as his custom was, he went into the synagogue on the sabbath day" (LUKE 4:16, KJV).

Of course, the holiest day of the week for Christians was the first, not the last. Christ rose from the dead on Sunday, not Saturday; and Sunday was the Lord's Day, not the sabbath. It was a day off, not for retreat but for Easter exultation. No disciple can sit still on Sunday, for he will be compelled, as were Peter and John that first Easter Sunday, to run and tell.

Gradually Sunday merged with the sabbath in Christian practice until the fourth commandment came to be applied to the Lord's Day. Charlemagne, in A.D. 789, decreed all ordinary labor on Sunday as a breach of the fourth commandment. Perhaps, as Professor David Freedman insists, Christians should revere Saturday for sabbath rest, which, the experience of the race confirms, our physical limitations demand, saving Sunday to celebrate our Good News.

Men break this command unconsciously, not because they have outgrown it, but because they cannot bear to face a day's reflection. Sabbath stillness is a vast assignment for men accustomed to escape in activity. How many of our problems might solve themselves, and how much of our lost selves might catch up to us if we took our God-given time at this sacred stopping-place!

*Honour thy father and thy mother* . . . (EXODUS 20:12, KJV). This directive was not necessary for children of a strict Jewish home; it was addressed to adults rather than adolescents. "Honour thy father and thy mother"—in advanced age. Ethics was invading virgin territory here, for so many early societies could not wait to sweep the superannuated out of the way. Both the very young and the very old were often fed to the elements, the gods, or the wild beasts. The fifth law let it be known that life was precious to the last drop, and obliged parents to protect grandparents from the dangerous precedent.

This requirement does not prevent the next generation from placing the aged in an institution. Honoring them means respecting their wishes and taking them seriously as long as they live. It surely does not mean forsaking God and the job of bringing up children in order to be devotees to an exclusive cult of caring for the dying. Some sons and daughters are forced to wait hand and foot on reigning matriarchs when they should be free to live their own lives uninhibited by pathologically long apron strings. Many mothers and daughters should be separated for the sake of both. Each family must find its own way along a fine line distinguishing between sick guilt and the will of God. A man must learn when to "*leave* his father and his mother, and . . . cleave unto his wife . . ." (GENESIS 2:24, KJV), so he shall be able to return his parents' love in the right way and not by doing blind obeisance to extravagant demands. A man must be responsible to God alone; he must not attempt to keep the Fifth Commandment until he has acquired the perspective accomplished by obedience to the First.

Perhaps this commandment is meant to instruct minors. But whose fault is it if youngsters are not taught to yield the floor or a chair to their seniors? Perhaps our age is paralyzing children with privileges and showering them with things to excuse gross neglect. How many juvenile delinquents fool their youth away destructively, feeding on scraps of comfort from a guitar or crusts of love from lonely girls pitifully trying to make up for a father's absence? How is any boy ever to put our Father in Heaven in the highest place of honor if he has never had a father on earth who loved him like a son? How much of the skyrocketing teen-age crime is a heartbreaking effort to make up for parental affection missing from the formative years.

No wonder Jesus mobilized us by the reminder that family responsibility goes far beyond blood. When the disciples once informed Jesus that His mother, His dear mother Mary, was outside waiting for Him, He corrected them emphatically: ". . . whoever does the will of my Father is . . . my mother" (MATTHEW 12:50, RSV).

*Thou shalt not kill* (EXODUS 20:13, KJV). Slaughter sears almost every page of the Old Testament; even the prophets were hardly pacifists. Captured cities were customarily massacred and eight out of nineteen Hebrew Kings were assassinated. The strict translation of the Sixth Commandment is: "Thou shalt not murder"—meaning the murder of another Israelite—so in the original this Command did not prohibit capital punishment or military conflict. The Creator of life does not appreciate a cancellation, and enjoins reverent conservation of His chief objective. But the blood of Cain still gushes guilt on our heads. The face of our despairing world is streaked with the spreading stain. War is destruction, presumably the very state in which God found the abyss the evening before the beginning. Creation is His intention to establish ultimate peace and order out of chaos. He has already gone so far as to sacrifice His son to assure us that the day is coming when this commandment can be kept in a happier kingdom where even the lamb shall lie down in safety beside the wolf and the bear.

Mercy killing may not be so merciful. If we were to permit it, then the patient would never know when his physician would become his executioner instead of his healer. Such a development would strain the relationship between doctor and patient. And yet we question the heroic measures of heart manipulation and massive transfusions that propel the human machine on and on after one's time has come. As the borderline between life and death becomes more difficult to define, we are not at all thrown back on our own ingenious devices, but more than ever on the mercy of God. Modern medicine, to keep pace with its gifts, must learn to surrender its services in fresh humility before the *special* will of God in each instance, or it must become an incredible disservice. By artificially clinging to physical existence, man may be killing the larger life. We cannot know how to apply the divine commandment without divine help.

Suicide is recorded only three times in the Bible, but it has recently become the third largest killer of teen-agers between fifteen and nineteen years old. Twenty thousand Americans died by suicide in 1965, and there were 200,000 *known* unsuccessful suicides. It is doubtful that Hamlet's dread of something after death, or that this commandment, would restrain anyone so friendless as to entertain that last resort. Something is radically wrong with a suicidal candidate long before he is pushed off the brink. Certainly others standing near that life's beginning are accomplices in any eventuality of slashed wrists. According to Dr. Viktor Frankl, a man who is suicidal may be identified by his literal inability to articulate any positive reason why he should go on living. Such a negative state of mind was not occasioned simply by circumstances beyond his control at the last minute. Someone stepped on that life at a tender age, predisposing the youth to despondency. The love and discipline the child received was so unreliable that he was saddled with pathological insecurity. Belief in God is a slippery business for a boy who could not trust the life his loved ones handed him. Suicides may be murder in disguise.

Christ went further. ". . . it was said by them of old time, Thou shalt not kill; . . . But I say unto you, That whosoever is angry with his brother without a cause shall be in danger of the judgment" (MATTHEW 5:21–22, KJV). ("There are two Greek words: The ordinary word *to kill* and the word *to murder*. And when Christ quotes that commandment He uses the *murder* word in all three accounts.") The act of murder begins in the brain, and anyone who has gone far enough to premeditate murder is guilty. "Thou shalt not kill"—neither with looks nor with longing.

*Thou shalt not commit adultery* (EXODUS 20:14, KJV). If the Fifth Commandment orders society around the family, the Seventh makes marriage the family tie. Time did not permit a textbook-length commandment, and when you tell the truth you do not need to justify it with fastidious terminology; so the ten commandments are a self-evident brief of the way life is, and originally were probably no longer than one word each.

Adultery originally meant sexual relations with a woman bought and paid for by another man; and so, when Sarah and Rachel could not have children, they innocently supplied their husbands with their handmaids. Marriage at first was a man's "keep off" sign on his property in wives; it meant so much more when Christ finished His definition of it. Out of the promiscuous mist, when men were at the mercy of animal spirits, an ideal became legible; a man's promise to a woman became precious enough to last for life. A higher law was entered on the books of consciousness which no man nor woman could break without abusing something unspeakably sacred in their own lives and in the hearts of their children.

Marriage *is* made in heaven. Only one Matchmaker can tie the knot that holds happiness " 'til death us do part." Is it so strange that the God, who made us unique, has someone in mind for each? A triangle is not true to life, and the paper chain of marriages which burn briefly remind us of the mistake of love's disorder. The deserted crones who in the end cannot remember which man they're married to, or where they put the children; the debauched, desolate, and unfaithful husbands to whom all women prove unfaithful, offer convincing confirmation of the divinity of the marriage obligation.

Mistakes are made in marriage; sins are forgiven, but this ancient rule continues to recommend a happier state. Christ agreed and pointed toward the mind, where danger strikes first. In this fundamental sense, the sin is in the blood, and there is no such thing as a man who needs no mercy here. "But I say to you that every one who looks at a woman lustfully has already committed adultery with her in his heart" (MATTHEW 5:28, RSV).

Christ's interior interpretation of this large order indicts today's soaring pornography industry. Pornography originally meant "a description of prostitutes and their trade," but now it envelops "writing, pictures, etc., intended to arouse desire" (*Webster's New Twentieth Century Dictionary*). Pornography has already leaped far beyond the illicit traffic in little books lying at the back of dark closets. The problem has almost overwhelmed periodicals; it dominates the covers, if not the contents, of the paperbacks, and has landed out loud in our living room. The film industry has survived TV by massive transfusions of sex. And what can the advertising man sell without a picture of a suggestively dressed girl?

Many who attack this menace of pornography are often unhealthy victims of repressed interest in the subject. Such fanatic censors also forget that "freedom of speech," as

Justice Oliver Wendell Holmes finally convinced the court, also means "freedom for the thought that we hate." Safety and growth not only demand a favorable environment but also more demanding self-discipline. The trouble, of course, with both sensuality and self-righteousness is that they are starved for the satisfying thrill of God's friendship. Sloppy fiction and jabbing fingers are sick substitutes for man's first love.

Jesus wished to defend us against the dry rot of any age's audio visual raids and the disintegrating daydreams to which they give rise. In any sin a man's mind goes first, which is why Jesus especially hoped to stop this sin there.

*Thou shalt not steal* (EXODUS 20:15, KJV). This statute safeguards private property. The Psalmist believed that honest prosperity was a proof of a man's merit, or at least of God's pleasure in him. It is not money, but "the *love* of money," that is "the root of all evil" (I TIMOTHY 6:10, KJV). It is idolatry, and not capitalism, that creates misers and pickpockets, and maintains the endless feud between the haves and the have nots. Wealth must be chastened with imaginative charity or become a partner in crime. We must learn to apply the wisdom of the admonition, "give to him who begs from you, and do not refuse him who would borrow from you" (MATTHEW 5:42, RSV)—or tempt the underprivileged to steal "his share." The world must become a place where robbery is rendered obsolete by ingenious thoughtfulness. Riots and revolutions arise from the failure of the favored to appreciate how much their wealth is a gift from God which they are to divide with dependents.

Theft is not simply a sin; it is also a compulsive sickness. Kleptomania may be one child's unconscious attempt to compensate for the lack of parental affection. This

Commandment, then, is broken, as in the case of suicide, by the gross neglect of parents. Who knows how much guilt for today's crime comes back home to roost, and how often the father or the man who could have helped should be sentenced, as well as the son. No police force can check the crime. It must be prevented by those who can keep the spirit of the law by taking more responsibility for each other. This commandment made Moses think of the next one: Thou shalt not steal someone else's good name.

*Thou shalt not bear false witness against thy neighbour* (EXODUS 20:16, KJV). The Bible loves the truth, but it is not as worried about little white lies as it is about slander. Specifically, the Hebrew verb in this law prohibits lying in court; stealing someone's glory or reputation is bad business that approaches murder. How many who would never think of picking a pocket, stoop almost daily to this ugliest burglary? The Bible abominates character assassination in the spirit in which Shakespeare denounced it:

> Who steals my purse steals trash;
> Tis something nothing;
> T'was mine, tis his,
> And has been slave to thousands.
> But he that filches from me
> My good name robs me of that
> Which not enriches him and
> Makes me poor indeed.

This Commandment concerns not simply the courtroom, but quite obviously includes the party and the backyard fence. Keeping this Commandment would kill the most common curse laid upon the race—*gossip*. A good man will bear witness only to what is good; no bad word about anyone will fall from his lips.

*You shall not covet your neighbor's house; you shall not covet your neighbor's wife, or his manservant, or his maidservant, or his ox, or his ass, or anything that is your neighbor's"* (EXODUS 20:17, RSV). The First Commandment goes to the heart of the law: Worship God only. The rest are on the surface of *do's* and *don'ts*, except the last, which plunges deep again into the secret heart where sin begins. It seems to say, "You shall not indulge in thoughts that could lead you to break any of the aforementioned laws." This breeding place of crime in the corner of the mind must be cleaned up; evil must be turned off at its source. Jesus made the most of this solution. The business of religion is not to repress evil, but to pack the house with good company, to produce a creative life by a clean mind. With Jesus' finishing touch, these Ten Commandments became enough to keep us out of trouble. They take us up to the threshold of what He called "the Greatest Commandment of all."

Proponents of the new morality claim that the Commandments may be broken in order to fulfill the higher law of love. True, the Christian idea is to do the unique will of God for each special situation, but God never needs to sacrifice principles to satisfy any situation. If we try to keep the Commandments even when they appear most inappropriate, God always comes through. Perhaps there are no exemptions. Maybe God wanted that woman to stay in the concentration camp; perhaps, later, He was going to open the right door to let her out. If God wants you to have a dime for an emergency phone call, you won't have to commit a crime to get it. God will stir a man to give it to you or help you to think of some other way. The laws stand and perhaps are most in force when we feel least sure. What are any laws good for except for those very occasions when we are being most tempted to abandon them? This God who thinks of everything is not served illegally; but He tailors His laws beautifully to every situation. And if we can hang on to the Commandments at the firy moment when we are certain that keeping them will ruin us, God will do His amazing part, just as He did for Daniel standing that night in the lion's den.

# 5

# The Great Commandment

JESUS TOOK THE Ten Commandments and turned them
into two. He did not destroy the laws of Moses but digested
them into one memorable statement that drove law home to
the heart where it belongs. "Thou shalt love the Lord thy
God with all thy heart, and with all thy soul, and with all
thy mind ["and with all thy strength," according to Mark
and Luke]." This is the First and Greatest Commandment.
". . . Thou shalt love thy neighbor as thyself. On these
two commandments hang all the law and the prophets"
(MATTHEW 5:37–39, KJV). Jesus pieced them together from
DEUTERONOMY 6:4 and LEVITICUS 19:18.

The Great Command does not eliminate the others.
Today's audience is different from the one to whom Jesus
spoke, for He was addressing men who didn't need to be
told the ten Commandments. Jesus' words were apropos of
a thoroughly familiar body of moral law, and His simpli-
fication and emphasis on the right spirit needed to be made
more for hair-splitters than for fence-sitters. The tedious
religious network of that day was crying for the relief and
fresh air that Jesus brought with Him. And while the Great
Command is apt also for us, our morals already stretch like
rubberbands. We are foreigners to the strict fundamentals
of Moses without which we cannot fully appreciate how

advanced a seminar in ethics is presented in this Great Commandment.

The Great Command does not assign more law. It attaches us to God, personally, in a relationship that is to be bigger than obedience. We are to *love* God with *all* that we have and are. Who comes first with you? God is nothing but a good word for the Unknown to so many so-called Christians, but behind morality and far beyond it breathes this amazing friendship. Before faith ever goes into action, it must get terribly personal with the Maker and Redeemer of all human relationships. Notice that this Command never strays near the subject of neighbor until *after* the love of God has been underlined.

Life with the Father means everything to Christians. The intimacy in marriage only suggests the burning intensity of a man's first love for the One nearer than hands or feet. Tragically, men sit sleepily in God's house, never in all the world expecting to make His acquaintance, contenting themselves with the repetitious reading of His old letters, instead of carrying on a dynamic correspondence as did David, and, finally, the One who taught us all to say: "Our Father."

A young man talks about nothing else but his girl friend. Yet, the remarkable One who gave him this girl friend is his best Friend, that One from whom no secrets are hid, the One who lavishes a perfect love more beautiful than the love of women. This is not a prejudice against the fairer sex, but the splendid appreciation of their Creator, our very own Father, ". . . fairer than ten thousand." This would be assuming the supreme obligation seriously. Who is the first one you think of in a triumph or a crisis? To whom do you turn first to tell your troubles, and who has the last word in your life? The Great Command demands that this be God, and we must admit that whoever else enjoys this preeminence in your life or mine really is taking our God's place.

Why? We do not have time to ask nor answer all the questions. We might just as well ask "Why love your mother?" Existence is a state of emergency, and the Bible is rushed for time. Life takes place in the middle of the night. Suddenly we are awakened, and we hear a voice telling us that this house of earth is afire, and we must leave with Him immediately or perish. We are tempted to ask questions and stall for time. "Who are you?" "How do we know if this is real and you are reliable?" The Voice replies, "Trust Me, and I will explain everything later. Have faith, come quickly, and you will be blessed." We can kill a lifetime in a never-ending argument of why and whether to "love the Lord thy God"; we are not forced into submission by conclusive evidence—that would make us puppets instead of sons. We are urged to gamble everything on God. "Ask not," said Augustine, "which is the Way. Rise and walk in it."

*With all thy mind.* . . . The Great Command is no obscurantist request for us to unscrew our heads and rest them under the pew. Jesus enlisted the comprehensive man; God made and meant our best brains to obey to the best of our knowledge: ". . . you will know the truth, and the truth will make you free" (JOHN 8:32, RSV). The love of God has nothing to hide or fear, and eventually we find, as Augustine confessed, that the very questions we raise against God were sent by God to bring us to Him. "The fear of the Lord is the beginning of wisdom . . ." (PSALM 111:10, KJV).

However, the debate about God can be a side-reaction to the chief objective, which is not only to know but to do the will of God. Scholarship can be, as Kierkegaard warned, a new and more insidious attempt to get around God. Down on the beach one day, Jesus addressed Peter, James, John, and Andrew very simply: "Follow me." This is the only way we can know who we are. We must read everything that will inform and articulate our belief, but the proof lies not in our mastery of complicated texts; it lies in the practical experiment we are conducting at heart. God is not dead to men because He does not exist, but rather man is dead to the reality of God. We say we do not pray because God is not real to us; yet God is not real to us *because* we do not pray. The noblest challenge before us, ultimately, in suffering and at death, is not to understand *why*, but to accept what must be.

Christianity is not a branch of learning, but a tree of being. Do not learn *about* Christ; *go* with Him. Press your whole mind into His defense. Our tutor is not the professor but the disciple, and our authority is vested not in any ivied seminary, but in the envied sainthood to which the scrubwoman may by grace be saved.

Tragically, we've learned the Great Commandment backwards. Many remember only the windup about the good-neighbor policy, but that conclusion can't be disconnected. We are only human, and we can't behave like brothers unless we first live like sons. Loving neighbor is a pretense without the prerequisite love of God. Without the tempering of God's love, the unloved mother's love either becomes possessive, smothering the son, or evaporates, stranding him in neglect. Without God, man and wife make too much or too little of their mutual affection, with disastrous consequences. Human relationships cannot stay healthy except through that divine subsidy of forbearance and forgiveness which the umbilical cord of God's love affords. So long as we are slightly unbalanced children, we shall need a Father standing by to step in and smooth things out; otherwise we shall pinch morals for our own ends, as do Pharisees and libertines. Love must be the servant of God, to use C. S. Lewis' words, or stoop to being a tool of our ulterior motives.

It was a great day when men recognized that God was sick of slaughtered sheep and sacrificial blood, when they perceived that His heart was set on His children loving each other. And this Commandment cannot permit anyone perpetuating any form of completely introspective piety. The prayers of petition, however conscientious, can't be completely heard except in company with those of intercession. In fact, God soon seems remote from those who've lost rapport with their beloved. The son alienated from his father often feels nothing for his Father in heaven. The bride unloved in the flesh loses her faith without extra outside help; and so, when friends desert us, we feel that God has, too. The love of God and neighbor are two sides of one coin, and destroying one destroys the other, for, "If any one says, 'I love God,' and hates his brother, he is a liar; for he who does not love his brother . . . cannot love God . . ." (1 JOHN 4:20, RSV).

This extraordinary Command makes the second mile mandatory. The Good Samaritan story is not a tract on how to keep up your neighborhood; it is a "must" to the deserted, helpless castaways of the human race. All the Samaritan saw was a battered body by the roadside, a man who needed help. The conversation surrounding funerals sometimes strays on how the poor fellow "never did anyone any harm." A driver of a hearse volunteered that one of the marvelous things he appreciated about a dead man was that he never yelled. Those comments may be superior to criticism, but they scorn Jesus' Commandment to have a care for the other fellow. Christ would be pleased to find neighbors trading sugar and borrowing flour back and forth, but His Commandment is far superior. His parable on the last judgment bears down hard on how much we love those who are at our mercy. The big question on judgment day will have to do with what we have done for the stranger, the naked, the sick, the prisoner, the forgotten man, the man our day discriminates against. They may be in our own house, or across town; wherever they are, that's our battleground. ". . . as ye have done it unto one of the least of these my brethren, ye have done it unto me" (MATTHEW 25:40, KJV).

*Love . . . as yourself.* The brilliance of this psychological insight has been lost to us. Its mature demand is made prematurely. We can't tell somebody to love others as he loves himself if he has no love for himself and never known love. A little child cannot share until he's known the pleasure of possession. No man can deny himself if he's known nothing but enforced denial.

An unloved boy sits in the counselor's office enthusiastically drawing monster pictures of his father, or pictures of himself shooting or beating his father. That boy is not ready to love God as his father or his neighbor as himself. He must express that bottled hostility first. If some teen-ager enters the conference room, shouting, "I hate my mother!" the counselor should approve, for probably that child has been carrying that buried grudge too long, and will not get rid of it until it has been sufficiently and heatedly ventilated. Someone insists that the daughter should love and forgive her mother. True, ultimately, but in the meantime she cannot be forced to pretend love and forgiveness without serious consequences to herself. So many persons are trying to follow the positive commands of Christianity while filled with negative feelings, and such malpractice produces neurosis. Their well-meant hypocrisy can split the personality.

The lad who was never loved at home in the right

way—something that so often happens when the home is divided underneath—needs to spend time in the permissive company of a father-figure, confiding all the ugly facts of his unhappy story with the utmost frankness. Having been robbed of a hearth, he must have this substitute where he is understood and not rebuked, appreciated yet not advised, until in that integrating atmosphere he truly comes to himself.

Only after a man has pulled himself together is he prepared to give himself away. Until that catharsis, he will only be able to put on an act of forgiveness, for deep down the repressed frustration and anger will sabotage him, and lash out in spite of him, to do others damage. He cannot let bygones be bygones until they've been thoroughly blurted out in painful words. As Dr. Paul Tournier has shown, God asked Abraham to leave his place, but that is something a boy cannot do until he first finds and savors his place. Self-sacrifice is the crowning Christian act, but it must not be exacted of those not yet equal to it. Some of us, it is true, are only too well prepared, and are putting self-denial off for the devil's sake, but others, who had never been permitted to express resentment because "it is not nice," must sufficiently exercise selfishness before they can throw self away. One should not be asked to keep his temper if he has been afraid to lose it. One must learn to love himself first, otherwise his love of neighbor is a disservice to both.

However, the time comes when a man must make a sacrifice. The cross came so bright and early in the life of Christ. We can only say: "Greater love hath no man than this, that a man lay down his life for his friends" (JOHN 15:13, KJV). Others are not asked to do that once and for all in death, but day after day. That lifelong assignment was the shining answer Christ made to the lawyer who asked. ". . . what must I do to inherit eternal life?" (MARK 10:17, RSV).

# II

# THE PILGRIMAGE

# 6

# Your Morals and Your Health

"MEN DON'T DIE, they kill themselves." Some scorn cigarettes as "coffin nails" and deride drinkers as "men of extinction" while they industriously dig their own graves with their teeth. Others, aghast at rich feeding habits, are dying from dieting and lack of sleep.

There is a stern relationship between a man's morals and his health. Temper raises blood pressure, and resentment speeds the pulse. Dr. Norman Vincent Peale has been accused of twisting Christianity into a physical fitness program; yet we have been warned to keep the Commandments, ". . . that thy days may be prolonged . . . in the land which the Lord thy God giveth thee" (DEUTERONOMY 5:16, KJV). The Bible warns over and over, "When I say unto the wicked, Thou shalt surely die . . ." (EZEKIEL 3:18, KJV). While life and death are supremely spiritual matters, they are also fleshly. The inner man pollutes or purifies the earthen temple that houses him. "My experience," an older man writes, "is that my physical health is in direct ratio with my moral and spiritual health."

Modern medicine reaffirms this long-standing diagnosis. Good or bad behavior does things to one's liver. A psychoanalyst declares: "Most illnesses do not, as is generally thought, come like a bolt out of the blue. The ground is prepared for years, through faulty diet, intemperance, overwork, and moral conflicts, slowly eroding the subject's vitality" (Paul Tournier, *The Healing of Persons*).

We are either breaking our health or rebuilding it, depending upon the immorality or morality of our life. We cannot cheat here without getting caught, for we shall pay in flesh and blood for our bad habits and dirty looks. No man can harbor resentment or stew in envy without suffering physical torment. Bad living ages a body just as moral regeneration makes a man feel ten years younger. The body registers the effects of its occupant's behavior, either inwardly bleeding from rebellion against God, or basking in His peace.

Take temperance in eating and sleeping, work and play. Drones suffer for their feather-bedding. No one is going to enjoy good health if he spends his life around the race track, relying on jackpots. The insidious fever of trying to get something for nothing, of counting big on some Bingo, contaminates the constitution; the person not integrated about a satisfying purpose withers and warps as a tree trying to grow in rock and darkness. You cannot snub the Commandment, "Six days shalt thou labour . . ." (EXODUS 20:9, KJV), without paying in bed sores or mental paralysis.

Overwork is another sin that makes us suffer biologically. We are all more tolerant of the man who is killing himself with work than the one who is killing himself by running away from it, but both extremes are immoral, and run up the rates of hospitalization insurance. A man can work his way to the hospital as well as to hell. The speaker may feel complimented when he is introduced as one who "works like a horse," but is that healthy for a man? Hyperactivity can be pathological. "He's a very busy man" may be an insult, depending on what a man is busy about—whether he works to avoid the emptiness in his soul, or to keep from having to sit down and think his life through on a Sunday afternoon.

What is one's work doing to the rest of the family? Overwork is often the work of pride. One mother slaves away to make herself indispensable, another to indulge a martyr complex. ". . . the seventh day is the sabbath of the Lord thy God: in it thou shalt not do any work . . ." (EXODUS 20:10, KJV). Overwork kills more Americans than cars do. We have become perpetual-motion machines in our frantic flight from God. A job was made for a man, and not a man for a job.

Eating and sleeping are now such battlegrounds that we forget what a turning point they can be for our physical well-being. Perhaps the art of pushing oneself back from the table, and the art of putting oneself to bed represent our most strenuous moral assignments. Part of the world is hungry, while the other half suffers from some phase of apoplexy; the starving are dying to eat what the stuffed are dying to share.

A friend of mine who had a coronary confessed that a team of heart specialists were not satisfied with what they saw on his cardiograms, so they combed his personal life to determine what had really caused his heart attack. They found that he had been coaxing a heart attack for years through his habit of bolting his food on the run. His blood was demanded suddenly in his stomach for digestion, and simultaneously in his head and feet for work, and that unfair strain finally showed.

A doctor gently but firmly informed a man who was trying to live two lives at once that half the patients in his crowded waiting room could go home right away if they would only eat right and sleep regularly. But they preferred his little pills to extensive moral reformation. How easily we hide our frustrations in under- or overeating, in too much sleep or sleeplessness, and with a death grip on the medicine bottle. Someone paces at night because of an unsolved problem; he protests that he forgave his enemy, or pretends to accept the death of his father, but deep down he did not. So he paces nocturnally, until he becomes a pushover for a bug that finally takes advantage of his lowered vitality.

One night at a College of Wooster Alumni meeting, the chairman asked the oldest member of the old guard present to rise and say a few words. J. Campbell White, grand ninety-year-old man of the lay missionary movement, and once a president of Wooster College, rose to claim the honor in a booming voice. He had played golf that week and had driven his own car to the meeting and his whole bearing was that of a vigorous man in his sixties. Someone asked him the question: "To what one fact do you attribute your health and longevity?" He answered immediately: "When I was a boy, another boy bullied and badgered me almost to the point of breakdown. I hated this boy fiercely, yet couldn't sleep for fear. Then I learned in Sunday school that Jesus taught us to pray for our enemies. Having tried everything else in vain, I prayed one night for God to bless my enemy, and I kept it up night after night until that boy became my friend. Ever since, I have made it a practice to pray first every night for the person who bothered me most that day and kept it up until the tension was resolved. I trace my health and long life to that single practice, for I never permitted any resentment to cost me indigestion or a minute's sleep."

One cannot be a Christian without turning over every detail of his daily life to God. Our children have nothing on us; we too need a Father to discipline our behavior behind the plate and on the pillow, and I have never known anyone who mastered these two basic matters without God's outside help. Grace ought to have something to do with temperance as well as thanks, just as the bedside prayer should say, "Thy will be done," about bedtime.

A man will jump from a window for fear of being found out or in sheer futility of finding a solution to his moral mess. A restless woman I knew was always buying beyond her ability to pay. Once she was caught embezzling funds from a civic organization of which she was an official. Through others' tolerance she was permitted to pay it back. She took a new job as an accountant and soon suffered from hypertension followed by a case of bursitis. She seemed increasingly furtive and jumpy. Late one night I was called on an emergency to her home. She was lying on the living-room floor. The life squad was working over her in vain. The coroner's report read, "Coronary," but I know better. She died from embezzlement, for after the funeral someone confided that she had continued her embezzling in her new job, and died just before being arrested.

A brilliant teen-age girl once went to see a counselor because she frequently shook and shivered for no apparent reason. She had been referred to the counselor because a test had revealed that behind her jitters lay some unresolved psychological problem. The girl told the story of her life, which included some very difficult childhood experiences. Finally, on the third visit, she began to talk about her father; it was very difficult for her. Her hatred of her father was so fierce that she wept with anger as she choked out the story. Once, father and daughter had been inseparable, then the father disappointed the daughter. Dad was not the man the girl once thought he was; he was her mother's mouse who meekly turned over his entire weekly pay check and everything else. Dad always answered, "Ask your mother," to his daughter's every request. The girl also saw that her father couldn't take recommendations contrary to his own wishes, and he always wanted to be left alone in any job. He never put in a good word for anyone else, and never listened to a word someone else was saying. "He's a 'basement man' who cares more about his beer and his hobby than me," his daughter said.

The day finally came when the girl's rejection of her father, which had been eating away at her vitals, came completely out into the open, and she recognized what was wrong with herself. One day, with tears rolling down her cheeks, she found it in her heart to forgive her father. That moral step ended her shaking.

A Boston doctor who runs a clinic specializing in the treatment of arthritic afflictions, concluded that more than half the number of arthritis cases have their origin in a moral conflict. Dr. Karl A. Menninger, in the *Bulletin of the New York Academy of Medicine* (April, 1938), stressed the "tremendous influence of the state of mind in the condition of those suffering from high blood pressure . . . thus high blood pressure often seems to be a sort of physical expression of a moral hypertension which parallels it."

Even accidents are not always accidental. The recent novel *Accident* goes behind a teen-age driver's crash on the highway into the long story leading up to that tragedy. The collision was no accident. The boy had been asking for it for a long time; in speed and almost studied carelessness, by every means except outright suicide, he had been indulging his death wish. Instead of facing up to his feelings of inferiority, he had fled from them, faster and faster; he was caught in the illusion of superiority he forced on his automobile, unconsciously carrying his successful friend in the "death seat."

I can trace the last two times I crunched my car fender. One time, while I was driving down a hill of ice, my wife informed me of a bill I felt to be unfair. My indiscipline settled on the accelerator, making us ride about ten miles an hour more than we should have been doing, and we struck a wall. On another occasion I was taking the children birthday shopping. We made an inordinate number of stops while the tension in my mind mounted. Finally one more stop was requested. "Not another!" Nothing happened until we pulled away from the curb, where I left the imprint of my impatience upon a parking meter and a rear fender.

It would be an oversimplification to ascribe moral problems as the cause of all so-called accidents, but in the cosmos of a Christian who believes that events are either providential or the devil's work, and not accidental, one is less and less likely to blame circumstances on that pagan god, Chance.

It is absolutely clear today, if not before, that our body answers to a good or bad conscience. We may slip over the words as though we could get away with murder, but this prayer is a matter of life or death: "We have left undone those things we ought to have done; and we have done those things which we ought not to have done; and there is no health in us" except as we come personally to terms with what we had better do before God. And unless we do God's will willingly, we won't get well. We may notice, along with the Psalmist, that some people apparently get away with misbehavior. Oh, no! The godless man who never misses a day of work may be the most likely target for the major disease that cuts him down swiftly. We are all human: no one is immune. The Perfect Man died young so that we could live long, not in the flesh, but forever with God. Sickness of mind and body is inextricably related to specific sins. Just as our battle for good behavior affects the battle of the "bulge," so does vexation give one woman a migraine and one man an ulcer. The incubation of diseases such as cancer, tuberculosis, and cardiac failure is not unrelated to the tranquillity of our inmost personal life. Whether our confidant is our grocer or our milkman (many of whom may have more understanding and loyalty than some professionals), we must not hesitate; our secret anguish or rancor is going to poison us until it's out in the open.

Confession isn't the end of it. Confession forces us to take some steps. A distinguished doctor declares: "There is no physical reform without moral reform . . . God has a purpose for every man . . . to depart from it . . . has harmful repercussions on health."

Mental illness now takes too many hospital beds. Some moral problems are preying on men's minds, driving them into distraction and despair. Those who have been loved possessively, or those who were neglected may be most subject to the unhealthy tricks the mind plays on us. Some people run away from an inferiority complex by boasting; the sick escape disguised as Napoleon. Others excuse themselves with a persecution complex, blaming a political party for their plight. Whether it is hysteria or schizophrenia, these mental aberrations are man's refuge from his moral failure to face what life demanded of him.

How can moral reformation reclaim a man's health and restore him to his rightful mind?

"When the great Dr. Sladen, with 140 doctors under him at Ford Hospital in Detroit, came to Pittsburgh to address the surgeons. . . . He said: 'Gentlemen, in medicine you and I must need in a day like this, when men are cracking up all about us, something more than you can buy in the corner pharmacies; we need a great grip on God.' Then he went on to explain. He said nine other surgeons and he, who had been appointed by the United States government, were asked to draw up ten laws of public health and give them to the American people. He said: 'We debated and argued from ten to twelve days and finally one of us decided, "Let's take the beatitudes of Jesus Christ." ' He said then, 'We cut the laws down to nine and we simply changed the word *blessed* to *healthy*, and we had it. "Healthy are the pure in heart," because sin is sand in the human machinery and it shakes a man to pieces. "Healthy are the peacemakers" because hatred brings about a schizophrenia and a divided personality inside us that tears us to pieces—in disposition, in health and in power. They had it, the laws of the Nazarene" ' " (Louis Hadley Evans).

When someone asked Dr. Karl Menninger, the prominent psychiatrist, "Suppose a nervous breakdown is imminent, what are you to do?" the physician answered, "turn the key in your door. Walk out across the tracks, find some people who need you and do something for them, and you'll probably ward off a nervous breakdown." It is striking to find a doctor administering a "prescriptive ethic."

There is more. Moral effort can't remake us. Recommendations and added responsibility will only imprison these patients deeper in their distress. The solution for the defeated lies in faith which is a gift of God which He may not give until a man is prepared by others' loving prayers and listening understanding. Health awaits the irruption of Jesus into a man's experience; and when that comes, Jesus will explain not merely, "Your faith has made you good," but rather, "Your faith has made you *well*."

# 7

# The Beatitudes

THIS TIME JESUS prayed all night. And as the sun was coming up, He summoned His disciples to distinguish twelve for special assignment, and to say some things mankind has remembered ever since as "The Sermon on the Mount." Luke said the sermon was preached upon the plain, and covered it in a chapter; to Matthew it lasted three times as long; but both men put it near the beginning of their books, began it with Beatitudes, and pronounced the benediction, "building a house on rock."

It is frightening, for Christ was so demanding. He delivered His Commandments as a Moses, but from a higher mountain. What He said created conscience, and still towers in unapproachable idealistic splendor: man's brief of perfection. This sermon should have been preached in heaven to angels, for men have been uneasy ever since they heard it. It has made living here more awkward; our best is not good enough. Sinners have killed themselves for forgetting it; saints have died from frustration, trying to live up to it. Others, drugged with earth, shrug their shoulders, shake their heads, and shout "Impractical!" and water it down into something else. Scholars excuse it as "interim ethics" to be used only until and if Christ had made a quick return. The church seasons it heavily, but it worries every man who has heard it, and it beckons him.

We must remember, this sermon is not the only thing Jesus ever said. The New Testament is crammed with checks and balances. Christ knew, too, how to use a whip, how to scald Pharisees with adjectives, but let us not be afraid to listen to His keynote address. We will not be able to keep up, and soon we will be out of breath, but if we can follow Him at all there may be a blessing, even as our last chapter promised, upon our physical condition.

"And he lifted up his eyes on his disciples, and said: 'Blessed are you poor, for yours is the kingdom of God'" (LUKE 6:20, RSV). This is where the Beatitudes begin. Poverty is not necessarily a virtue; it can come from being lazy. But the poor are so pitiful, and there are so many of them. Jesus wanted them to see their advantages. Poverty protects a man from the deadly curse of pride, and educates one to stop, look, and listen for God. Men will find happiness sooner in serving than in being waited on, yet Jesus did not damn prosperity. This blessing is addressed to the poor; not for the well-to-do, to justify their oppression of the poor. The secret of the Kingdom is not in rags, He said, but belongs to those who will become like little children—to "the poor in spirit" (MATTHEW 5:3, KJV). No man may enter into this sacred mystery until he recovers a child's aptitude to laugh, to marvel, and to embrace hope eagerly.

"Blessed are you that hunger now, for you shall be satisfied" (LUKE 6:21, RSV). Empty stomachs are not always a sign of piety, but the men to whom Jesus spoke were hungry. And so He insisted that God was not teasing when He made our appetites. Go ahead and ask for bread; but don't stop there. "I have meat to eat that ye know not of" (JOHN 4:32, KJV). Starvation's not a sin, not permanent; man's soul is bigger than his stomach. Hunger is a vivid illustration of homesickness for "the land more large than earth, more kind than home." Famine reminds us that restless "Man shall not live by bread alone . . ." (MATTHEW 4:4, KJV). Luke put this precious poetry down just as it came from Jesus' lips, but man needs Matthew to interpret: "Blessed are those who hunger and thirst for righteousness, for they shall be satisfied" (MATTHEW 5:6, RSV).

"Blessed are you that weep now, for you shall laugh" (LUKE 6:21, RSV). What? Jesus Christ shocked sadness with His smile. He was not untouched by our disillusioning procession of funerals; He saw before Him all the downcast faces of all mankind, all the days of their years drowned in tears. He saw in their eyes these words unsaid: "Is this all?" But He did not slap backs; He discerned a treasure hidden beyond death.

It is only in the darkness that one can see the stars, that one can see how much he needs the hand of God, and how far the love of God will go. God is going to be especially tender to us in hard times. Take them in good faith, and don't be bitter or afraid. Blessed is the man who cries over his sins, for tears can be an oblation to God. Man ought to take evil seriously and swallow hard for his brother's shame. There is a time to "Weep with those who weep," but wailing is not the last word. Rather, it is an excavation of the soul to make room for the surprise of "joy that seekest us through pain." The mother of all miracles was born in a grave. "Blessed are those who mourn, for they shall be comforted" (MATTHEW 5:4, RSV), at last, with happy laughter.

When Matthew counted his blessings he found four that Luke forgot.

"Blessed are the meek, for they shall inherit the earth" (MATTHEW 5:5, RSV). It took a strong man to admit this Beatitude, for most men feel too weak to take their physical strength so lightly. Cowardly lions are afraid to act like lambs; but meekness does not mean a Milquetoast. It means "terrible"! The French make *debonnaire* of it. Christ was not admiring mice, but men who are mature enough to let God have His way, and strong enough to smile at themselves. Since they believe in God, they need not rattle their swords nervously. They rest secure in surer fortifications, trusting God to provide for them amply in His will.

Cynics snap under the nerve-racking strain of looking out for themselves. The scramble for privileges and the job of self-promotion condemn men to hard labor, for it is God's work. The meek have no trouble keeping their minds on their work. They leave the rewards to God to give, and they can live lightheartedly. Earth is not to be the prey of our ambition. God is so extravagant a Giver that His humble servants are forced to cry, "Enough! My cup runneth over!" "He hath put down the mighty from their seats, and exalted them of low degree" (LUKE 1:52, KJV). *Blessed are the meek, for they shall inherit the earth.*

"Blessed are the merciful, for they shall obtain mercy" (MATTHEW 5:7, RSV). Weak men cannot endure pity—for someone else. The guilty get relief by punishing goats. But this Beatitude's a blinking red light: "The punishment you give, you shall receive." The court of life is honest—in the end. "For your heavenly Father shall not forgive you until you forgive your brother from your heart." That is the verdict.

Society itself is hardest on the hardest heart. So heaven will throw the book at perfectly decent Pharisees. We shall not always be sitting safely in the jury box; our turn to take the witness stand is coming. We will be judged, not only by our mistakes, but by the severity of our judgments on the crimes of our fellow men. The devil will have to help the man who is not merciful; God will not.

The merciful are too mindful of their own mistakes to be hard on their neighbors. Any man who has peeked in the mirror by Biblical light will gasp like the publican: "God be merciful to me a sinner" (LUKE 18:13, KJV). He will not be quite so quick to condemn some thief hanging by his side; and in that stretch of earthly patience, he will win heaven's pardon. "Blessed are the merciful," He said, "for they shall obtain mercy."

"Blessed are the pure in heart, for they shall see God" (MATTHEW 5:8, RSV). Jesus had a Galahad in mind, not a Lancelot, a knight of virtue far above our boorish Broadway version. The pure in heart are those faithful to God first, *in everything*. They can look Him in the eye. They are men who, though tossed by the storm, stay constant as the compass needle, for their "delight is in the law of the Lord . . ." (PSALM 1:2, KJV).

This blessing is very hard *for* us and *on* us. Our motives are mixed up with many masters; our childhood innocence has been defaced long ago with furtive looks and thoughts. Our hearts, if not our hands, are guilty of almost every conceivable crime. Only the clear-eyed, the clean, will get to see God; but we are redeemable. A Friend gave blood to baptize us so that we too might stand one day, blameless, beside the saints, to behold God's majesty. "Create in me a clean heart, O God; renew a right spirit within me" (PSALM 51:10, KJV). These words should bow a head or two, but they should also make life sing with promises again: ". . . though your sins be as scarlet, they shall be white as snow; though they be red like crimson, they shall be as wool" (ISAIAH 1:18, KJV). Here is hope that we will know once more how happy it is to have nothing to hide.

This text is an advanced assignment, but how kind of Him it was to speak these promising words to men like us: "Blessed are the pure in heart, for they shall see God."

"Blessed are the peacemakers . . ." (MATTHEW 5:9, RSV). Peace is not the pregnant stillness before the battle; it is more than friction's absence. Peace is not a truce, but an offensive of tranquillity. This is why He came. He was announced: "The Prince of Peace" (ISAIAH 9:6, KJV), and His angels anthemed: ". . . on earth peace . . ." (LUKE 2:14, KJV). "Peace, be still," is what He said to storm and soul (MARK 4:39, KJV). It was His last bequest: "Peace I leave with you, my peace I give unto you . . ." (JOHN 14:27, KJV).

Peace must be made, and it must be made with God first. Peace is reproduced from affirmative patience and understanding, and these come from Christ. Revenge is so much sweeter. Peace positively runs uphill against hell's downdrafts. Peace is a preventative, pouring on the smoking embers of prejudice and jealousy, smothering the smoldering grudges, and drenching the ashes of old hatreds before they can ignite again in violence. It takes courage and obedient vigilance.

Peacemaking is God's work. It gives man an apprenticeship, and makes him a kindred spirit God adopts.

"Blessed are those who are persecuted . . ." (MATTHEW 5:10, RSV). Our idea of heroism is not a martyrdom. We don't like second-rate, sophomoric deaths on our stage. We prefer our Messiahs to die with sword in hand and steaming hot with another's blood. The very idea of persecution makes us shudder. Christ disagreed. Persecution is a priceless privilege that should make us "leap for joy" if done for righteousness' sake (LUKE 6:23, KJV). Those who die drugged in bed don't know what they are missing.

But "beware when all men speak well of you." Your loyalty to the cause will eventually make enemies on the other side. ". . . so persecuted they the prophets . . ." (MATTHEW 5:12, KJV). You cannot be good without paying for it. Yet "Blessed are you when men hate you, and when they exclude you . . . on account of the Son of man!"

(LUKE 6:22, RSV). Was He only fooling? Will God reward His casualties with something more precious than purple hearts?

In T. S. Eliot's play, *Murder in the Cathedral,* the Archbishop of Canterbury couldn't wait for his turn to die. He said, "I have had a tremor of bliss, a wink of heaven, a whisper, and I would no longer be denied." Fear of death is such dismal nonsense to the dedicated. This doomed man seemed glad, and cheered his trembling disciples: "I am in no danger, only in the presence of death. . . . Death will come only when I am worthy, and when I am worthy, there is no danger." "Blessed are those who are persecuted for righteousness' sake, for theirs is the kingdom of heaven" (MATTHEW 5:10, RSV).

# 8

# Monday Morals

DO OUR MORALS get up with us on Monday morning? Should they stay up as late as we do on Saturday night? In some cultures, a moratorium is declared on behavior for the duration of a festival. Is misconduct at the annual office party as inexcusable as during business hours?

Christian morality wears work clothes; it does not pose in its Sunday best. To us morality is the very practical matter of how one operates in the back room when no one is looking. Our morals are values so vital they cannot take time off. This code of honor is carried on in the jaws of the most extenuating circumstances, foreign and domestic; it extends to the way one treats a competitor or a client.

Winston Churchill was said to have asked an actress, "Would you marry a man for a million dollars?" "Of course," came the reply. "Would you marry one for five hundred?" "Of course not! What do you think I am?" "We have already established that, my dear," said the great statesman. "Now we are only trying to determine the degree." The woman had her price.

A Christian does not have his price. Morals are valuable by definition, and any man who values them will die before sacrificing them. Morals mean that a man has established a point beyond which he will not go at work or at play. A soldier friend of mine during World War II could not bear to leave his buddy bleeding on the field; he died bringing his friend in to safety. A doctor should die before deserting the dying. It were better for a preacher to die than to preach lies or pap. An attorney should offer his life before accepting money to pervert justice. Would it not be better for a businessman to die before being paid for a disservice?

A fair bargain is a better deal than charity. A bartender decided to have some fun with the old Methodist minister walking down the street, so he flaunted a ten-dollar bill in the preacher's face as he came by. "Pastor, I suppose you wouldn't take ten dollars of the devil's money?" Quick as a flash, the minister snatched it, without changing step. "Certainly, the devil's had it long enough," he said. While God can redeem the filthiest lucre, God is more interested in how the bartender gets his money than how he gives it away.

There's nothing wrong with making money. John Wesley preached: "Earn all you can, save all you can, and give all you can." The church has been constructed from poverty-stricken saints, but it also rests on affluent pillars like Abraham, Joseph of Arimathea, and John D. Rockefeller, Jr. T. S. Matthews frowned on his own socially prominent family for scorning their neighbors, the Proctors, for being "in trade," but working for a living was never an indignity to men whose chief Apostle made tents, and whose Master labored as a Carpenter. Robert Frost said, "All I insist on is that nothing is quite honest that is not commercial . . . nothing is true except as a man or men adhere to it—to live for it, to spend themselves on it, to die for it" (*The Letters of Robert Frost to Louis Untermeyer*). Money is not tainted. It is the love of money that is tainted. Mark Twain defined tainted money as "'Tain't yours and 'tain't mine." A dollar is innocent until men make it almighty.

Certainly it is bad to be in any business that profits at the expense of people's welfare. We object to the sale of olive oil adulterated with a filler which permanently disabled its consumers in Algeria. Who can recommend making parachutes that won't open, or washable shirts that won't wash? It is stealing to misrepresent or misprice any commodity. Wherever we go from here, who can defend price-fixing, padding expense accounts, or not keeping one's part of a bargain?

Recently one drug firm cut down on research and pushed for the release of a drug, thalidomide, on the market. Dr. Frances Kelsey of the Food and Drug Administration refused to license its sale in the United States for lack of sufficient data on its testing. The drug firm exerted every kind of pressure to secure approval by a steady stream of phone calls and by going over Dr. Kelsey's head, but she would not give in. Soon heartbreaking evidence began pouring in from abroad on the ill effects of the drug. Some of the babies born to mothers who had taken the drug were dead, or had malshaped legs or flippers for arms. Thanks to the moral courage of Dr. Kelsey, who received the President's Award for Distinguished Service in 1962, this disaster did not descend upon America. There was one line of integrity the doctor would not cross. Business must attend first to God's business, or become the devil's work.

Dr. Marshall Scott, a recent moderator of the United Presbyterian Church in the United States of America, told of several high-ranking executives of a national tobacco firm who were requested by the company to study the cancer research relating to the use of cigarettes, and then to develop a defense to demolish such charges. Their research convinced the executives that cancer and cigarettes actually were related. Understandably, two of these men might have felt forced to resign immediately and a third might prick his company's conscience from the inside, but no one could be excused for taking this information sitting down in church on Sunday and going back to work on Monday to a business that was burning out hearts and lungs. Dr. George James, New York City Health Commissioner, testifying before the Senate Commerce Committee in Washington, D.C., said that two thousand New Yorkers died in 1964 from lung cancer caused by cigarette smoking. "This means that cigarettes were one of the major agents causing death in our city last year." (Christian Herald, July, 1965). Could anyone believe this and remain morally neutral? Imagine America's wrath if cranberries had caused an epidemic of two thousand deaths.

There is more to a Christian businessman's morals than restraint. The purpose of a Christian in business is not service to make a profit, but profit to make a service. If a man is in a job only for what he can get out of it, he has missed the point of the job. If life work means no more than a paycheck, it is a pity. The purpose of life is not to make a killing; the purpose is to produce. We are for free enterprise, but trying to sell something useless to someone just to make a fast buck is poison to our system.

A man is not a Christian if he is not most concerned about doing an honest day's work in the best way he knows how for a product on which he himself is sold. Gibbon said that his tutor "remembered he had a salary to receive and forgot he had a duty to perform." A man who works with his eye on the clock is a waste of time. A doctor who cares more for his fees than for his patients, a politican more interested in power than in good government, a minister more interested in his people's purses than their souls, are all bad businessmen.

Is it possible for a businessman to be Christian? Granted, that is a formidable assignment, but is it not more difficult for a minister to be a Christian? He is paid to be used by

God, and yet he is powerfully tempted to use God. The clergyman can even call on the sick for what he can get out of it. Can a church be Christian? How many churches pay their benevolence with money robbed from their own janitors' salaries or their ministers' pockets? An institution's charity is a crime if it is not first generous to its own employees. It is dead wrong for the minister to get rich off the church, but it is also wrong for the church to take the attitude of the old deacon who prayed for the new preacher: "Lord, You keep him humble, and we'll keep him poor."

Assembly lines and cybernetics are often martialed as fresh excuses for businessmen not being able to be Christian any more. A huge computer was fed the question: "Is there a God?" The monster soon spat out the answer: "There is now." But the machine is not responsible for our dehumanization. It is man who walls himself off in a high-rise hermitage, insulating himself against the shrieks of someone being raped down on the streets. Such tragedies are not due to the time, but to men whose fathers had the same trouble back in Carthage; they suffer from the same affliction of self-possession that infected the travelers on the road from Jerusalem to Jericho.

A physician was introduced to a distinguished colleague he didn't recognize and later found he had walked by her desk every morning for years. His excuse was not the giant size of the hospital, but that his eyes were on the floor. A case could just as easily be made for machines making it possible for deeper personal relationships than those enjoyed by Daniel Boone, whose nearest neighbor lived forty miles away by horseback. Working on an assembly line may not be the ultimate in excitement, yet Brother Lawrence found God in the so-called drudgery of pots and pans. Sir Winston Churchill distinguished himself by the little acts of thoughtfulness illustrated in his remark to the corner bobby: "John, how's your mother?" Personal attention is not at the mercy of our IBM voting categories, but at the mercy of every single man. How can our multiplying labor-saving devices, new leisure time, and longer lives be excuses for depersonalization?

A friend of mine came from a good family, went to the right schools, and found himself president of a small toy firm. Then a malignancy in his lung required a critical operation, and he was given only a few months to live. Miraculously, he acknowledged God and completely recovered. As a protest to his friends' enthusiastic Protestantism, he went in for Oriental religion and reverently took the Lotus position every night. One night he noticed his little daughter playing with a lump of wallpaper cleaner, so he colored it and marketed it as Play Doh. He made a million dollars with it the first year. He still signed his letters to me "The Dali Lama of Cincinnati," and during the wave of incendiary suicides by monks in Southeast Asia, he signed: "The Only Buddhist Afraid of Fire." But in between the lines of his exciting life, he felt the gentle pressure of the hand of God. He did not, as do some insensitive tycoons, assume credit for his success. Three years ago he said, "I have become a Christian," and the next spring his voice on the other end of the line stunned me: "I am phoning from the New York Toy Fair. I feel called to go into the ministry." That fall the *Wall Street Journal* reported that he had sold his business and entered a seminary.

God makes our business His business if we let Him, and there are many men like this man who have been blessed enough in one adventure and are ready for a bigger one. This is when life goes beyond a livelihood to become a living.

There is nothing wrong with bringing home the bacon, but life is bigger than stockpiles of bacon. The biggest thing in life is what we take from home, not what we bring home. Michelangelo didn't do what he did for bacon—bacon wouldn't quite cover the Sistine Chapel ceiling. When Luther said, "Here I stand, I can do nothing else," he was not being paid by the hour. Pension rights were not a part of Washington's winter at Valley Forge; in fact, George Washington wouldn't take a penny for his military services. You can't pay someone to be a father to his country.

"Money never manned a lifeboat." The Coast Guard captain was speaking to all the world's employees when he reminded his rescue crew: "We *have* to go out; we don't have to come back." It is as though God were saying, "You keep your mind on your work, and I'll remember mine." Remember the Young Man who died on the cross. He was doing something for life, for others, for which He could never be paid back.

Yet that cross occasioned a resurrection. Any man who gives his life to God, who spends it at God's wish, will be paid a bequest of blessings compared to which his salary will seem a fringe benefit. So often, the big bottleneck in a good job is the puniness of the purpose; adopting a better reason for being busy brings the Kingdom right in to the same old shop. God will take care of the hard cash, too, but only divine employment, to use Samuel Johnson's words, can ever make one "rich beyond the dreams of avarice."

# 9

# The Seven Deadly Sins

THE WORD *SIN* may stand for a mess of mistakes, but it makes most men think of only one. Dorothy Sayers said that a young man once confessed to her: "I did not know there were seven deadly sins. What are the other six?" *Lust* is definitely one, but only one, of seven notorious killers. We do not want to exhaust our horror on this one scandal, as backdoor gossips do, nor swing to the opposite extreme and brush lust off lightly. So let us get a good family picture of the nest of sins on the classic blacklist of the church fathers.

Alfred Kinsey may have made lust look sweet and innocent, but she's still our bitter enemy. Sex was in God's garden before the snake came in, but every good thing is bad apart from God, and lust is sex perverted. Lust is illicit greed, and breeds an abnormal addiction to the body, fixing life in the bottomless rut of that one request. Lust cripples everyone remotely connected with its rage. Lust lives with treason on the rampage with the ego. It is obnoxious to security and venomous to love.

Any triangle, however temporary, any outbreak of this sin in the heart of a man, clouds the life of his wife and tightens the laughter of his little children. Lust is robbery, and takes the heart out of housekeeping. It starves all of life's other functions, strangling that first purpose we are, above all else, designed to serve. Slowly lust sneaks each ideal and dream into its orbit. She makes her subjects lick her boots until no son could look up and say, "That's my dad," and no father could point with pride and prayerful thanks because "That's my boy." Lust is love's cancer and deserves to die, but men must cry heavenward for scaffolding to carry that well-meant resolution.

Add *anger* against us. She's another summer-seeming sickness that can be fatal. Both lust and wrath make their prey temporarily insane, supplying loads of extenuating circumstances. Lust misleads a man to believe he's broadminded and undergoing a more mature involvement; fury is convinced it suffers solely from righteous indignation.

The riverboat captain is not the only offender. Hostility can wear impeccable velvet gloves. Who has not seen the squinting face of a vicious dowager working in vain to conceal the diabolical mania that is about to explode on behalf of the Society for Something or Other? The straw boss lashes out in scalding sentences at the intolerable inefficiency of his fumbling office help; some wife spits in apoplexy over her puttering husband's hopeless stupidity. The tirade pours out poison-pen letters and stinging rebukes, belching a lava of abuse in which to boil some innocent bystander who coughed. Rage knows no reservation, no magnanimity; all is bottomless black. Eradication, not justice, it requires. The tantrum will not stop short of hounding someone to death and doing a "savage war dance on the body."

The news media are unhappily aware of this vice and its insatiable craving for delicious fuel. "Nothing pays so well in the newspaper world as the manufacture of schism and the exploitation of wrath. Turn over the pages of the more popular papers if you want to see how avarice thrives on hatred and the passion of violence. To foment grievance and to set men at variance is the trade by which agitators thrive and journalists make money. A dog fight, a brawl, or a war is always news; if news of that kind is lacking, it pays well to contrive it. The average English mind is a fertile field in which to sow the dragon's teeth of moral indignation; and the fight that follows will be blind, brutal, and merciless" (Dorothy Sayers, *Creed or Chaos*).

Now is no time to be lukewarm nor to lose one's head. The man with his wits about him will refuse to be swept into the vortex of emotionalism. He will not see red at the first difference of opinion, not because he does not have an opinion, but because he believes wisdom will not die with him. He will stand for something, but will not be sidetracked into trying to be heard above the din of everybody else trying to be heard. God's man will not rush to conventional defensiveness; he was doing something while nobody was doing anything. And when everybody gets into the act, he may step back and pick up precious things mislaid in the publicized shuffle.

The clear head is meant for something more resourceful and imaginative than heating collars and hitting ceilings. Christian behavior today will not cavil, nor be merely civilized; it will be temperate. Equanimity means that we will react to foul play without a vengeance, preserving the perspective the lynch mob lacks. Our sin yesterday was in doing nothing, and our temptation today may be in trying to make up for everything all at once. Now, while everyone is talking at once, is the time to remember that God gave us ears. We do not jump to conclusions, but make them come to us. Christians are concerned, but not incensed; active, but not trigger-happy. Bringing in true brotherhood demands level heads and lawful means. We can no longer afford the primitive luxury of hysteria. Sober Christians cannot allow themselves to become tools of one plot pitted against another plot, such as the Civil War. We seek the golden mean between apathy and exasperation; both sloth and madness are deadly sins. Brotherhood is not a last-minute crash program, but our life's work. We go at it not passionately, waving red flags, but compassionately, walking on palm branches.

*Gluttony* is also guilty enough to get on this black list, yet slick enough to receive more laughter than tears. While lust enjoys the spotlight, gluttony is getting away with murder. Bay-windowed pastors bury sex under an orgy of denunciation while busily burying themselves in flesh. If the devil can't provoke a clergyman to sin in wrath during the sermon, he'll catch him off guard a little later in the more formidable temptation of a chicken dinner. While TV is rightly condemned for its bloodthirsty violence, no one notices the man of distinction doing his disappearing act. America's worst problem plagues us all from the highchair: How to push ourselves back from the table. "The belly," as Don Boyce reminds us, "is the king of the passions."

Gluttony goes on from there. We go hog-wild over some craze: if it isn't the Beatles, it is birds or souped-up stock cars. Moderation somehow escapes us Americans. We get hooked on integration or states' rights, fire prevention or conservation, till we can't talk about anything else. We can't take it or leave it; we take it as hard drinkers, heavy eaters, bookworms, or golf-a-holics. We drive like Jehu and smoke like chimneys. Even our schools and universities are not always founts of wisdom. Some of them have become pie-eating contests to see who can devour the most pages the most quickly. Our children are force-fed facts until they come out their ears, nursing in the rest of us the absurd illusion that if youngsters are gorged on information they will come out educated.

Calvin noticed that curiosity can be lust. Subtly our culture is absorbed in a frantic dead run for more facts until no time is left for us to make friends. We only have time to choose sides or manipulate people into whatever drive we're heading up.

Gluttony gradually gives way to *covetousness*, and it is very difficult to distinguish where one leaves off and the other begins. However, something terrible is happening to the all-American boy in his hunger for the top. We are not safe from avarice if profit is more important to us than the product. "Going places" definitely does not mean going to the right place. Making a pile of money was not the main purpose of Paul's life. We poke fun at mad chemists, but the mania for self-advancement and vainglory plagues all the professions, and that approach is far behind the Bible's. God called one man a fool for building bigger barns to no purpose except to stuff them with his own surplus. The avaricious man may never stray so far as Silas Marner, but if his life is mainly devoted to affluence, or to seeing the youngsters through school so he can enjoy a pension, then a villain has him by the throat. God preserve any pressure group from gaining the whole world and losing its own soul.

"Gregory the Great placed envy among the seven deadly sins. . . . The covetous man wants to possess the good of his neighbor. Whereas the envious man . . . regrets it. He grieves over his neighbor's good luck. That is why John of Damascus called envy a species of sorrow and defined it specifically as 'sorrow for another's good' " (W. F. May, *Christianity and Crisis*, January 7, 1963).

We don't mind admitting that we get mad or eat too much, or even that we looked at another woman; that makes men look manly, human. But we'll be shot before we'll confess to being green-eyed; that is a mean, cold-blooded sin. And if avarice is the temptation of the haves, *envy* is the temptation of the have nots.

According to La Rochefoucauld, "Few are able to suppress in themselves a secret satisfaction at the misfortunes of their friends." Dr. W. F. May reminds us, as Aristotle observed, that envy flourishes nearest home: "Let Pablo Casals be praised for a stunning performance and I am not likely to feel envy, for I am neither an octogenarian nor a cellist. Let someone, however, publish an article on envy while I am writing this article (as, indeed Angus Wilson has done,) and I am likely to know the subtle pressures of this sin" (*ibid.*). So the Bible records how envy broke out between brothers and colleagues: Cain and Abel, Joseph and his brothers, Jacob and Esau, and the older brother and the prodigal son. Remember how Saul envied David? As soon as David slew Goliath and became the darling of the people, it is said, "And Saul eyed David from that day . . ." (I SAMUEL 18:9, KJV). The Latin word *invidia*, from which our word "envy" comes, means "eyed," or literally, "to look upon."

Another's happiness catalyzes envy; jealousy simply cannot rejoice in another's good news. Jealousy dislikes laurels on another's head and is a debunker of its immediate superiors: a man's wife must not appreciate anyone else but him. Envy will read the worst interpretation into a colleague's success. It damns its competitor with faint praise and derives no enjoyment from his satisfactions. Envy calls a courageous colleague "crazy," a religious brother "naïve," a kind act "strategy." Envy wipes out the gracious deed with a word of disdain, and wastes no time in *thank you's*. It is no surprise that it was Judas who debunked Mary's gift of expensive perfume. No wonder envy is malicious and holds maneuvers.

Our nation now knows how Saul felt because Russia is giving *us* a run for our money. How easy for us to want to pin the Reds against the wall with Saul's javelin. Our society pits equals together for more savage competition. Put a batch of high-school valedictorians in the same college freshman class and you are bound "to get some Sauls." The mind of the "also ran" is a fertile seed-bed for envy. The Communist Socialist Republic was a triumph of a bitter working class over a bloated nobility. Envy and avarice together bred the French Revolution and guillotined thousands. Envy is not an outsider in today's struggle. Those who have must beware of the heavy-lidded sin of avarice; and those who have not must salve the sharp-eyed sting of envy.

*Sloth* is the madness at the other end of wrath. Sloth is complete insulation. In the world it is called "tolerance"; in hell it becomes "despair." It is the sin that believes in nothing, seeks to know nothing, loves nothing, hates nothing, lives for nothing, and only remains alive because there is nothing it would die for. Sloth assists and punishes all seven sins. Even hyperactivity does not slay that spider, sloth. All the alarm clocks and clogged calendars simply show vacuum under pressure. Sloth conceals her corpses in a web of deceitful smiles. There are those who think she is the easiest way out. Actually it is the hardest way back. Only God Himself can raise men from such a sleep.

All seven sins lie down in the sin of *pride*, the prolific mother hatching this litter. Jesus didn't dally with pride's six children; He went straight to the source of evil. Pride is the villain in almost all His Parables. It is the sin of so-called good men, and strikes where one smugly assumes himself to be strongest. If a man is law-abiding, he may substitute the law for God and become a legalist; if a man is a liberal, he may make integration his God; if he is a conservative, he may pray to the Bible. All our achievements stagger along the razor's edge of this gulf of "egocentriloquism." We are subtly misled to think: "The Kingdom's not coming, we're bringing it in!" The Communists tried to abolish the job of God and substituted atheistic five-year planning. Yet we search our textbooks, newspapers, and plays in vain for the impression here in America that God is alive and active. One seldom meets God in reputable print or popular shows any more except in profanity. A headless universe is presupposed in history texts. According to current events, God stays out of our way in school, business, and Broadway plays. Pride, the lizard-like insinuation that we're in this life alone and on our own, has opened the floodgates to all our misery.

Pride was the devil's only trouble. Lucifer didn't run around, he didn't overindulge; the only thing wrong with Satan was that he wanted God's seat. Cunningly, pride leads us to think we can get away with illicit love, for we see ourselves as better than the average bear. Pride blinds us to our biting avarice, spawns our cutting envy: "I am number one." And once God's gone out of our lives, we are sitting ducks for whichever substitute comes alone: Bacchus or Aphrodite.

As soon as the prodigal returns, pride is ready for him. Now that he's behaving, he'll face the sin to which his elder brother succumbed while staying home: the belief that he's a little bit better than the unreturned prodigals, or those with darker skin, or deadbeats who don't attack the problem as he did. Our voting record, our stand on an issue, our intellectual achievements begin to impress us with their superiority. More and more we are amazed at how lovely our life is—how courageous, how sacrificial, how noble!

Why can't other people see us as we do? Why can't they work as hard?

If others would only help us, join us, agree with us, everything would light up. The people on the right or left of us seem so stupid or sleepy. Then we're caught in a most vicious vice: our prayer, if we'd expose our attitude, is that of the Pharisee—"I thank God that I am not as other men, Republicans, Democrats, segregationists, integrationists, law breakers, law lovers. You can see, O God, how I alone am left," etc.—and on and on. Of all people, *we* are trapped.

Our only hope is that poor tax-collector praying over there. He knows how badly he's infected, how much he needs God. He can appreciate that somebody else may be right. A humble man does not have an inflated sense of his own wisdom; he will think twice before saving the world his way. A man on his knees will be a good influence for peace among his friends who occupy uppity antagonistic camps. He will not be so absorbed in the "only" answer, but in the only God. Take a look at this hero Christ held up for all of us to be: "But the tax collector, standing far off, would not even lift up his eyes to heaven, but beat his breast, saying, 'God, be merciful to me a sinner!' I tell you, this man went down to his house justified rather than the other; for every one who exalts himself will be humbled, but he who humbles himself will be exalted" (LUKE 18:13–14, RSV).

# 10

# The Four Cardinal Virtues

"CARDINAL" COMES FROM the Latin word meaning "the hinge of a door." Four virtues have been ordained cardinal, not only by Aquinas but by almost all civilized men. *Prudence, temperance, justice,* and *fortitude* are the hinges on which the door of good behavior hangs and swings. Three more "theological" virtues usually join this holy company to make the battle equal against the Seven Deadly Sins: they are *Faith, Hope,* and *Charity,* which come elsewhere between these covers.

Prudence has not been a common Christian name since Puritan times, and while it smacks somewhat of timidity, or a charity too carefully curbed, we hasten to restore it to a respected position on the necklace of Christian ethics.

Christianity has been criticized for being reckless and impractical until the world is only too well aware how easily goodness can act the fool and scarcely ever mentions charity in the same breath with common sense.

Contrary to this, Jesus proceeded, with the most business-like dexterity, to match childlike faith with veteran cunning: ". . . be ye therefore wise as serpents, and harmless as doves" (MATTHEW 10: 16, KJV). The majority of Jesus' parables could be classified under the department of economics, and in the story of the Dishonest Manager He demonstrated with jarring clarity His utter admiration for a man with a good head on his shoulders. Just because Jesus made the heart so important, that never meant He had mental reservations. He demanded "all thy mind"—brains adroitly added to blood—fully appreciating that His cause could never prosper without the sharp eye and canny "know how" misappropriated by the underhanded. His pilgrimage could not put up with sloppy players: "And the master applauded the dishonest bailiff for acting so astutely. For the wordly are more astute than the other-worldly in dealing with their own kind" (LUKE 16:8, NEB).

Americans usually associate sound investments with the bank; but a bank can go broke, and "thieves break through and steal" (MATTHEW 6:19). A wise man prudently puts savings second to saving men. One notorious Scriptural money-maker decided to rip down big barns and put up bigger ones in which to cram his surplus, but God interrupted: "Thou fool, this night thy soul shall be required of thee . . ." (LUKE 12:20, KJV). Banks stress discretion, and bankers dress conservatively to demonstrate how safe they are: "We have been in business since. . . ." Wiser men remember the shifting sand that occasioned a crash in 1929 when mighty Wall Street crumpled. The shock reminded some of the Panic of 1893; it makes us suspect the solidity of Ft. Knox and the pretentious child's play of insurance. Men who deposit their whole trust in an explosive institution may be as mistaken as misers misusing their mattresses.

The church of Christ has been in business for more than nineteen centuries, declaring that dearest of all questions to prudence: ". . . what shall it profit a man, if he shall gain the whole world, and lose his own soul?" (MARK 8:36, KJV). Blue chip stocks and bonds are not so firm a ground on which to make a stand. "Therefore whosoever heareth these sayings of mine, and doeth them, I will liken him unto a wise man, which built his house upon a rock" (MATTHEW 7:24, KJV).

*Temperance* is not strictly teetotalism from alcohol, nicotine, and coffee, although that may be one of its applications for many of us. However, the classic virtue of temperance must not be confused with one abstainer's list of contraband. Buddha, John the Baptist, and Mohammed were the harsh asceticists; the Son of man came eating and drinking. In all fairness to our irridescent faith, temperance means moderation in everything from books to bedtime.

First appreciate the beautiful sense of proportion in life that temperance wins. A good man can drown in a good viewpoint, just as a rebel can lose his perspective in defiance, or a mother's boy can surrender to cowardly acquiescence. A temperate man is not lukewarm, but he is above being reactionary or fanatic. His heart belongs to no camp or dogma, but to the living Christ; so he can manage a more mature attitude. He is concerned but never consumed, dedicated but not transfixed, sure of his ground but never too sure. Through all the alternating blasts of hot or cold, he refrains from jumping to conclusions or being pressured into taking sides. Such a man will not mistake a church nor a standpoint for God, nor will he identify his defiant brother as the devil.

The intemperate man, like the infant, lacks a finer sense of proportion. He cannot wait for what he wants, and will not look at the other side. Everything is all black or all white, all good or all bad. His town is the center of the universe, and his profession chief. Such a life is not complicated with practical exceptions to the rule, so it is quite opinionated. The intemperate man enjoys no insight on his own slant. He resembles the man in the asylum, obsessed in doing one thing perfectly. Remember Dickens' demented doctor who cobbled shoes incessantly in his cell night and day till he dropped? Our suspicious nature, off balance enough, can interpret every laugh or whisper as part of the plot to do us in.

A temperate life is a high art of avoiding extremes, of developing one's capacity to change while still holding "fast to that which is good." Emily Dickinson observed:

> Capacity to terminate
> Is a specific grace.

Temperance is the occupation of the peacemaker. Temperance does not simply reconcile antagonists, but also resolves impulsive conflicts into a well-rounded whole.

One's menu is ultimately an individual matter, for what seems to be one man's meat is obviously another man's poison. No Christian has the right to do what he is expected to do; he had better do what is best for him, determining his position from day to day, and in all things, by prayer.

The *Christian* question is, "What effect does your influence have on others?" Timothy might insist that his example of drinking a *little* wine would be the key; or more important, that his example of doing God's will for him would catalyze another man to do God's will in his own situation (for we are not to duplicate our brothers, but are to be obedient sons of the Most High). Paul told the Romans: "It is good neither to eat flesh, nor to drink wine, nor any thing whereby thy brother stumbleth . . ." (14:21, KJV). Would we drink if by so doing we would tempt a guest or tease a wife? What about the children?

Compulsive drinking curses more Americans than alcoholism. How many parties would be ruined for how many people if the bottle were taken away from them? There are not many who can take it or leave it; it is not unusual for a homecoming commuter to hit his driveway, secretly counting more on that cocktail than the kiss of his wife. So many people are drinking now that our time needs to be reminded that it is no sin not to drink. Obviously, the misuse of liquor is the *symptom* of immaturity, but when I have been called out at night to the scene of an accident involving teen-agers who have been carefully "taught how to drink"; or when I have heard the sobbing on the other end of the phone because someone's husband went home with someone else and hadn't come home for the longest time, I have wondered how much wishful thinking there is in letting liquor off so lightly. Almost every moral mess among the sons of the Puritans is first carefully bathed in alcohol; and the solution is so often complicated by its continued intrusion.

Even the first drink is not always snow-white. A lovely socialite once advised me how to drink in moderation in the right circles. Then, late one dark night, by telephone and from the vantage point of heartbreak, she volunteered that she was certain her husband's affair would never have begun without the influence of those first few sips—one drink, and he was not the man she knew. And, of course, the onerous challenge for the most judicious drinker is: How to drink without increasing the dose as the years go by? For if one five o'clock cocktail suffices a man for a lift in his twenties, it takes two in two more years to yield the same effect; and before he knows it, he's having one at noon. Beyond that point, if not before, drinking becomes a problem.

Jesus and His disciples drank in the fellowship of Christians, although they drank wine; Scripture has nothing soft to say about strong drink. But drinking wine at the supper table in divine companionship is far different from the brutal mob-drinking bouts men best each other with in the godless territory of icy shoulders and strident voices. Much of America drinks defiantly now, as though it couldn't care less what God thought, or as though it derived masochistic thrills from flaunting the encumbering guilt. Jesus turned wine into a sacrament identified with the blood of His sacrifice, but today the alcoholic sea of beverage is set up for a quick getaway from God; it has become the devil's sacrament of self-indulgence. The temperate man may drink only that wine blessed to make glad the heart.

*Justice* means fair play, and one would think we would have long outdistanced that fundamental by this time. Hardly! So far there has only been one Honest Man, and the rest of us are having as excruciating a time with honesty as with that keenest Christian virtue, humility. Some merchants may be so dishonest as to don "honest" nicknames to get you to buy questionable products from them. There was a degree of integrity among us unknown in some other countries, but time seems to be erasing the discrepancy. True, the minister of an American church in Caracas, Venezuela, lives in a lovely house protected by bars; he has been robbed three times in his fifteen-year pastorate; his mail has the same chance of getting through to him as the Pony Express, and cars parked across the street from his church are commonly hijacked for tires. Yet no one in his right mind would leave his keys in his car in one of our finest shopping centers here in America. Hotels with the finest clientele are forced to chain TV sets and fasten pictures to the wall. Honesty is a hard item to hang onto in the thick of the black market when there are actually policemen on the force, lawyers in the court, and witnesses who will accept bribes. Who are you and I to talk at income tax time?

Honesty is also difficult to define. The honor system may perpetuate a sin if it demands that a student squeal on someone he sees cheating. It is very wrong to steal help. Is it as wrong to give help? Is it not a virtue to refuse to tattle on the holy grounds of "Judge not"?

Injustice at its worst is robbing citizens of the ballot box because of their race, and equally abhorrent if a proper Bostonian enjoys more favor from a Board of Admissions than a bright farm boy from Indiana. Thank God, *fair play* is the cry of our age! Brotherhood is a study in justice so there may be no discrimination in the subtlest respect. An honest brother does not simply tolerate; he takes his brother in, whether or not he has a criminal record, and regardless of the color of his skin. A man who is condescendingly favored is denied the happier seat we save for the regular fellow. The Negro wants a chair, just like the rest of us, not a segregated throne. The crippled foster-child in *Room for One More* bragged to the boys about his introduction to spankings: "Sure makes a feller feel reg'lar, don't it?"

Friendship, at its best, requires candor. Confidences are afraid to emerge except in complete honesty, and no couple will enjoy each other's company long if they keep busy hiding things. Friendship will not be fooled into existence. An affront of intimacy paralyzes rapport. Poker faces may not give away any secrets, but keeping secrets after Christmas has come and gone gets the best of us. This conspiracy of silence freezes friendship and raises the guard without either side knowing why. One may not know what the other person is thinking, but he is profoundly disturbed or blessed by it. A bosom friendship is made by the unbearable heartaches and happinesses abandoned and accepted there.

The relatives may think they do the patient a favor by keeping the truth from him. Nothing could be further from the truth. What he doesn't know *will* hurt him, terribly: "Keeping something from him only sets him imagining all sorts of frightening but unlikely things." Anxiety shakes the man in the dark, and nothing relaxes him like the whole inside story. The truth cannot be perpetrated on a patient who is determined not to know, and the greatest tact and delicacy are required in timing the facts of life; but telling the whole truth and nothing but the truth is compulsory if the patient is ever to find the solid ground of peace. The sick man and his soothers may partially succeed in thinking they are fooling each other, but the deception multiplies the dread for both and very likely may show its hand in delirium under the anesthetic. Only ultimate honesty between nations, races, and partners will ever clear the air enough to make welcome the cure of love.

The annals of man are filled with acts of *fortitude*. This was the first virtue to win mankind's respect. Bravery on the field of battle thrills us still down to the very boots of human history. In this classic sense it calls back memories of Homer's Greeks who fought with gods, of the feats of Achilles, of the Spartans who died to the last man to hold the pass at Thermopylae. As savage and as bloody as this concept of courage is, it is glorious with the sacrifice of men for others. And when we enshrine in our memories the men at the Alamo, or those who raised the flag at Iwo Jima, where, it is said, "uncommon valor was a common virtue," we pay tribute to far more than the triumph of bravery over fear. We express awe for selfless devotion to comrades in arms, like that of the four World War II chaplains who gave their own life belts to others and went down with the ship, singing, standing arm in arm. Courage excites the poet as nothing else. Robert Frost pursued it everywhere. A friend told Frost of a very young soldier he saw being shot by the enemy. The scene kindled Frost's imagination and tears flowed immediately. Frost was consumed with the question, for he asked it over and over again: "Was he brave?" Frost's eyes shone when the answer came: "Yes, he was very brave." Courage was virtue's illustrious mother.

Yet there is a larger courage, with no time limits, which we call "intestinal fortitude." G.I.'s say "guts," meaning an endurance test through long day after long day. It makes us think of the heroes who grit their teeth against the relentless siege of that Goliath, pain; or of soldiers fighting the ravages of darkness and silence, such as were sent against Helen Keller. It is this vast kind of stamina—required of one the first thing when he awakens, and the next day and the next, as he grows older, weaker—that crowns courage with its brightest glory.

This brave spirit blends into faith, and into the finer meaning of all four virtues, which is not to *do* something virtuous, but to *be* virtuous. "There is a difference," C. S. Lewis said, "between doing some particular just or temperate action and being a just or temperate man." A poor tennis player can sometimes put a good shot over; what we are after here is the development of a moral quality that guarantees a high level of ethical performance. God is not after people who will do good occasionally, but He wants good people who can be counted on to come through because their habit of right living has become ingrained righteousness. King Arthur could practically depend on Lancelot to land the first blow and be the last to leave the field. Tennyson's graying Ulysses calls from each of us this last full measure of devotion:

Some work of noble note may yet be done
Not unbecoming men that strove with gods
. . . . . . . . . . and though
We are not now that strength which in old days
Moved earth and heaven; that which we are, we are:
One equal temper of heroic hearts,
Made weak by time and fate, but strong in will
To strive, to seek, to find, and not to yield.

# III

# THE TRIAL

# 11

# Immorality's Pet

"JUDGE NOT." Who doesn't? Fingers have been jabbing at each other ever since Adam blamed the apple on Eve. Busybodies are on the phone or in the barber's chair, handing down delicious opinions thick and fast about somebody else's case. Judgment ignites in gossip, whips into scandal, and ends in lynching someone's reputation. The meanest man inside us makes it his business to size someone up, then render the verdict to an enthusiastic jury of beady-eyed bystanders. "I don't like to say it, but I'll tell you what I think of old so and so," and then behind his back, or, better, to his face, we get out our yardsticks and let him have what Homer called "The windy satisfaction of the tongue." A scared man brands a darker skin inferior, a prejudiced northerner decides the white South is dirtier, and from the poisoned pen of some distant uncle comes a deluge of condemnation and free advice upon a nephew. Is there anyone who has not stooped to damn someone with faint praise or dismiss him as "adequate"? The newspapers are printed from the profit of it. The United Nations and political parties give priority to identifying each other. St. Paul himself found the most common curse of his churches to be *backbiting*, and this is the sin most mentioned in the New Testament. It is immorality's almost irrepressible pet, for it is cuddled and indulged by men who assume they are moral.

"Judge not." Why not? Outsiders don't have the evidence or the inside story. All that spectators can see of a ship in distress is the broken mast. They cannot tell who's to blame—whether the deck was awash through carelessness or by an act of God. A husband at war with his wife comes to a minister; the minister is wrong to rebuke. Even after he's heard the wife's story, he does not have enough facts, nor does he have the right to take sides.

A study on morality must despair of pinpointing immorality on someone else. "What's wrong with that man over there?" "He's sleeping." "He's sick." "No, he's pouting." "Why, it's a famous scientist thinking." All the self-appointed referees were wrong: Louis Pasteur was praying. An ancient Indian proverb stays our shafts: "Withhold criticizing thy brother until thou has walked for two years in his moccasins." By then a critic will bite his tongue. ". . . man looketh on the outward appearance, but the Lord looketh on the heart" (I SAMUEL 16:7, KJV), and the heart is too advanced a subject for biased bystanders to probe.

We not only don't have the pertinent facts, but we are incompetent to umpire another's morals. The famous five blind men of Hindustan debated loud and long, trying to make head and tail of an elephant. The one on the trunk end took it to be a snake, and the one near the leg swore it was a tree. We, too, are as blind as could be, and we swiftly switch what we see into what we want to see. Psychologists see through us clearly enough now to know that our critique of our competition reflects us much more accurately, for we like to cut down to our size those we fear or envy. When was the last time you complimented someone in whose presence you felt inferior? The man who lies is suspicious of another's honesty. A doctor once prescribed divorce for a couple simply because of their Rh factors; it followed that that doctor was in the process of divorcing his wife. Guilty men grow greedy to fasten guilt on others, or to read others into their predicament. If we feel we've failed with our children, we won't miss any mistakes our friends make with theirs. So the face of the lynch mob is unlovely with projected feelings. "Judge not"—because we don't know what we're doing. Remember how *we* crucified God's own Son as a common criminal!

"Judge not"—for judgment boomerangs. The more critical we are, the more critical others will be of us. If we frown at life, it frowns back. If we are looking for trouble, we'll find it looking for us, and in the end we'll be forced to drink our "Cup of Scalding." "Blessed are the merciful: for they shall obtain mercy" (MATTHEW 5:7, KJV). Cursed are the merciless, for they shall receive no mercy. The pound of flesh Shylock craved from Antonio was finally carved from him. ". . . with what judgment ye judge, ye shall be judged: and with what measure ye mete, it shall be measured to you again" (MATTHEW 7:2, KJV).

"Vengeance is mine, . . . saith the Lord" (ROMANS 12:19, KJV). "Jesus Christ shall judge the quick and the dead . . ." (II TIMOTHY 4:1 KJV). Judgment is heaven's job and none of our business. In the parables of the tares, the owner stops his hired hands from tearing out the tares for fear they would uproot good grain. "Wait," he counsels, "and at harvestime I will. . . ." Now is neither the time nor the place to tally up another's score in ethics. That is up to God in His own good time.

Then what *are* we to do? Judge ourselves. The court of our own conscience has enough back cases to occupy our attention till doomsday. There is, of course, the case of someone chronically running himself into the ground, pathologically feeling guilty for the unforgivable sin, but souls are usually smothering under exaggerated self-defense and retaliatory accusation. An embarrassing amount of time is consumed in keeping our reputation repaired with carefully executed chips off the block of our identical twin in the parable: "The Pharisee prayed thus with himself, God, I thank thee, that I am not as other men . . ." (LUKE 18:13, KJV). We're dead wrong. Our business is to take blame. Jesus in His parable of the last judgment anticipated the element of surprise on that blinding day when God decides to turn on all the lights. The goats were unaware that they deserved hell. The smug little Pharisees' song in *For Heaven's Sake* strips us: "I'm lily white, and clothed in light, and deaf, and dumb, and blind." Self-judgment is our homework, so we won't be so shocked when we take our stand that day in utter nakedness beside the blazing throne.

Inside each man is a howling storm of ulterior motives which give his virtues a twist and disease his ideals. We are bundles of brittle nerves and brooding desires. It is dark inside man; only the dead don't know it. You and I belong to a race of fallen creatures, each mind crawling with wretched contagion. If this is not true, then there was no need for God to go to all that bother about a Saviour. We have only to glance at today's headlines to see that the Good News was no oversight.

Better yet, stare into the neglected corners of our own eyes. It was the striking evil in their own hearts that impressed the saints with the sense of sin. The average man distracts himself by harping on the bad shape the world is in; preoccupied by the evil outside and around him, he raves about the crime wave and the juvenile delinquent. The godly man is more ashamed of his own little world. St. Francis, who could have sermonized incessantly against the evil steaming on the streets of his day, prayed instead: "Nowhere is there a more miserable sinner than I."

The news shrieks over the evil of scoundrels, the New

Testament unmasks the villainy in so-called good men. Jesus' parables were not on the corruption abroad or downtown but inside: "Lord is it I?" "It is I." The eleven never laid their blame on Judas; they left that to God, afraid that what was wrong with the world was their own fault.

Two things struck me upon a recent visit to a meeting of Alcoholics Anonymous. The first was the humility of those reconditioned people. Here was no pretentious society trying to impress somebody else; here was humility's golden hospitality. Nobody present was put on the spot. There was plenty of psychic air for all to breathe. One man stood to give "the pitch." He did not proceed to condemn the others for the way they were. He incriminated himself instead. Without any finger waving, he buckled down to the business of confession. That strategy created a mood of understanding. His was no high-pressure sale; rather he disarmed his listeners by being man enough to admit he had not been equal to the demands life made upon him. He didn't boast about being a sinner; he divulged his helpless foolishness; and after that courageous admission, the others felt relieved and free to let down their defenses.

The final objective of that A.A. leader was his testimony. When he had reached the wall and had gone down in utter despair, he cried out for help, and God arrived with His ministering angels. Ever since, he has been lighter on his feet. In the Bible, such an address would be placed in the psalms of praise.

Accepting blame and giving God credit is one of the New Testament's best-kept secrets. Peter's sermons were fired by the confession of his treason at Calvary, and he was one fisherman big enough to conclude with the old, old story of how *Christ* had done the pardoning and the rejuvenation.

Our time has come to step down from the superior air of

condescending insinuation, remembering Him who "like a sheep that before its shearers is dumb . . ." (ISAIAH 53:7, RSV), and, dropping to our knees in penitence, praying that others by His holy example shall be struck to the heart for their own sin, and that, out of the mercy they receive, they too will have mercy.

# 12

# Good Deeds Not to Do

IT IS TAKEN for granted that doing good is a great idea.
Everyone assumes that Christianity is a business of "good
guys" dealing in general good deeds. Who could question
the conviction that it is better to help than to hurt, and more
blessed to give than to receive? The church, we presume, is
definitely a total loss in time and effort unless it does something constructive in concrete example. ". . . faith without
works is dead" (JAMES 2:26 KJV). And we don't believe
there could be a good man who is not also a Good Samaritan; other examples will occur.

So far so good, but it will not do to leave the good life
like this. You know the story of the Boy Scout who helped
the little old lady across the street against her will. Saints
preserve us from such well-meant but misguided chivalry as
Don Quixote carried on! Quixote interrupted a beating and
bawled out the cruel master so roundly that after Quixote
got out of sight the rascal beat his slave with redoubled fury.
After the poor victim escaped, he begged Quixote: "For the
love of God, Sir Knight-Errant, if you ever meet me again,
though you may see them cutting me to pieces, give me no
aid or succor, but leave me to my misfortune, which will
not be so great but that a greater will come to me by being
helped by Your Worship."

Remember the man in the stalled car who requested the

woman driver to push his car at thirty-five miles an hour? Then he looked in the rear-view mirror and saw her bearing down on him at that rate of speed. With friends like that, who needs enemies?

There are so many "good" deeds that should never have been done. Can't we recall having done a kindness to show up a person? That was a dirty trick for which we need forgiveness. Have you ever humiliated a recipient of your charity by such an oppressive show of generosity that it only emphasized his feelings of inferiority? I wonder if there is anyone who has not caught himself taking the coward's way out and giving money to an alcoholic? Getting rid of him by giving in to his request is not necessarily charitable. Didn't you ever perpetrate something sweet that was resented? Old Earth has seen a veritable pestilence of fake friendliness. Ruskin's mother was said to rule her house with "inexorable kindness." And goodness can be saccharine as well as heartless.

Much of the record of Christian benevolences is besmirched by ineptness, imperfect timing, or mistakes. How many times have the best things been done in the worst ways? How often has a despicable thought propelled a beautiful deed? Is our good deed done compulsively to prove our independence from a too-dominant father, or to defy a wife or a husband who does not understand or satisfy us? Is our stand artificial, forced, man-made, or heaven-sent? Why did we speak out so vehemently in favor of the Red Cross? Because we felt guilty for not having done something else? Or were we over-reacting to expiate a shame in our domestic lives? Why did we accept a post in the Community Chest drive? Because we are uncomfortably well off? Because we want to pass for men with connections, or to pad our brochures? Why did we make that last hospital call? To keep from being criticized? To get credit? To show our proficiency and heart-rending pity? Or to *minis-ter?* This last is the reason we tell ourselves we did it.

This is not double-talk; it is the straight-from-the-shoulder talk of our Book. This mystery of mixed motives is the deep water of God's judgment and the matter of our life and death. God doesn't give a fingersnap for our demonstration of kindness. The best of deeds can be disguise. We see the motions men make; God sees the motives that make men. The unfeeling, unthinking exploitation of goodness is devil's work. The Lord is not looking at our well-manicured fingertips: ". . . the Lord looketh on the heart" (1 SAMUEL 16:7). You and I cannot get away with doing good *per se*, for God is backstage, absorbed with the vital statistics.

The New Testament describes a number of decent chaps going down the drain. Jesus watched do-gooders laying weighty tithes in the Temple treasury, as though they were playing horseshoes. He was not impressed. ". . . they contributed," He said, "out of their abundance . . ." (MARK 12:44, RSV); they never missed it. The poor widow's two coppers meant something because they meant everything to her; they were all the living that she had. I don't suppose there ever lived men superior to the Pharisees in behavior. That fraternity expertly made exactly the right move and always came up with precisely the right answer, topping it off with a tithe of ten percent of their salaries. Those fellows couldn't be topped in spiritual stunts, but Jesus blasted their goodness in scalding language because their goodness was an imposition. They were loveless and ugly-spirited inside. "Though I speak with the tongues of men and of angels. . . . And though I bestow all my goods to feed the poor, and though I give my body to be burned, but have not charity [love], it profiteth me nothing" (1 CORINTHIANS 13:1, 3, KJV).

Good deeds die when we put the cart before the horse. A man cannot act like a Christian until he becomes one. He cannot do good until he feels good by God's forgiving grace. One is not supposed to give something away until he gives himself up to God, otherwise the deed will be stamped with a petty desire to be paid back, "to be seen of men," or some other ulterior motive. That hand is unblessed whose head is unbowed.

We are unfruitful vines; every project our fingers touch withers; every high idea is frustrated, and all the best-laid plans are futile writing in the sand until we first fall into the hands of the living God. Without God, the good turn or the moral life is lifeless, unenlightened, scatter-brained, and uninspiring. No effort, no matter how worthy, is worth anything without being animated by a heart broken before God. We cannot do any good until that prerequisite Good has done us over, in one way, once and for all, and in another, day after day.

There is no more ridiculous burlesque than someone trying to force God's hand. Flinging silver carelessly in the lap of need, dumping surplus on despondent shores, or slopping off our charity from barren, unrepentant hearts and lives still obstinate and unredeemed, is the height of folly. It is the glaring reason we are not gaining in this mad race with death. Unless we are living on the lifeline of God's will and love, never forgetting that man shall not live by bread alone, our bread is stone. The only thing we have to give is the love of God given to us. In this spirit, our bread becomes sacramental, our money loses its taint; both giver and receiver are doubly blest.

Once our life has been offered to God, we give at His discretion. We do not decide what to do, or where it goes, and then ask His blessing.

Our happy privilege is to pitch into the particular assignment God specifies for us to do. This is so for a church, as for every single soul. There are a thousand and one bewildering possibilities crying for attention; we can and we must give priority to the ones so definitely ours, it is as though our names were written upon them. Once a man's heart is broken before God, his next move becomes as plain as day. It dawns on him in prayer that the people he has been pressuring and manipulating for his own purposes are names and faces to be cherished instead. Someone you've been holding off with fruitcake wants your complete attention. You will not be interfering, forcing, or fabricating your good works, as a busybody does; beginning with God, you will be led to a new thoughtfulness for your husband or your wife; and you will go on to a bright new relationship with your children. If God finds you picking up the threads here, He will open up door after door of specific opportunity for you. A twice-born man is not simply released into a general sea of helpfulness; he is detailed to a special mission. Such a life will not rob Peter to pay Paul, but will multiply blessing on everyone.

One needs not only God's wisdom to distinguish which deeds are his, but God's strength to execute them. A good deed is not a do-it-yourself kit. A good deed employs our first cardinal virtue to develop sanctified imagination and hallowed intelligence. Christians maintain a reputation for being charitable, but not so very sensible. As we have shown, we are seldom accused of prudence in the execution of a kindness. But the excellence we see in Christ came from the most reverent application of all the resources at His command.

To begin with, our deed is too big for us to do alone. We are not to do it *on* nor *for* as much as *with* someone. We need help to know how and when as well as what the deed is. Timing, patience, persistence are not our *forte*, but

God's. We won't accomplish very much reading the paper while our minds are somewhere else. Kindness is absorbing; it takes the kind of ideas only a loved one would think of.

Being Christian is not simply a matter of being business-like and efficient; a Christian must thrill with the agony and the ecstasy of a runner who has put everything into the race. This is how we approach our "more excellent way". This is why we build another's house as though we were building for ourselves. Our good deeds must be done with that finer eye that detects what the theatrical glance would miss and only the solicitous love of God would discern.

The man in whom there is no guile never goes out of God's field of gravity or debt of glory. Whatever else defines Christian love, there is an aroma of humility about it, and we can always detect a faint but burning incense reminding us so clearly but ever so gently that "Every good and perfect gift is from above . . ." (JAMES 1:17, KJV).

# 13

# Pre-fab People

EDWARD R. MURROW once asked Dorothy Thompson to name the most significant book on the shelves of her immense library. She brandished Aldous Huxley's *Brave New World,* which depicts the massive hypodermic that modern technology may administer to human life in the near future and in the name of progress. Being blown to smithereens by a nuclear blast is nothing compared to the job our own scientists could do on us in the process of making life painless and efficient. Plato's *Republic* and Thomas More's *Utopia* may still be remote, but George Orwell's *1984* is not very far away now.

Huxley's *Brave New World* begins with the words of a sign above a squat gray building: "CENTER LONDON HATCHERY AND CONDITIONING CENTER." In the name of economy, everybody in this future world is no longer born, but decanted; not bred, but compounded in batches of test tubes in that grim laboratory. All births are rigidly preconditioned to conform to four intelligence levels so that everyone will automatically take to the jobs the state intends them to perform. "Alphas and Betas remained until definitely bottled; while the Gammas, Deltas, and Epsilons were brought out again, after only thirty-six hours, to undergo Bokanovsky's process." This means that the Gammas, Deltas, and Epsilons were standardized in sets of identical twins. Baby Deltas had the love of flowers and books terrorized out of them by electric shock, while a love of drudgery was repetitively drummed into them, permanently imprisoning them in a static satisfaction with their preassigned factory tasks. One rack of test-tube treatment turned an embryo forever into a childishly happy "Gamma minus machine minder!" What could not be preconditioned by the computer's selection of chromosomes was subsequently controlled by oral brainwashing or injection.

Such talk is no longer science fiction. A life-size edition of the book that horrified Dorothy Thompson is bound to take shape for lack of a better solution to our problems.

Dr. E. S. E. Hafez now uses hormones extracted from pregnant mares and pregnant women to make a cow's ovaries release ripe eggs in quantity so that one hundred eggs may be fertilized and temporarily incubated in a rabbit until transferred to the womb of the final host. "Thus a whole herd of superb, pedigreed cattle could be transported easily and cheaply across oceans in a single rabbit while the mother grazes contentedly back on the farm" (*Life*, September 10, 1965). Mass insemination of supermen, a dream of some ambitious dictator, is well within the realm of possibility. Think of the temptation this will hold for coaches of professional football teams, or for the genius-greedy campus. "It is thus not absurd," wrote one of *Life* magazine's distinguished editors recently, "to imagine the day when a single tiny cell taken from the skin of the world's greatest genius might be grown into a second individual who is in every respect identical" (*ibid.*). In fact, such a man could be duplicated by the hundreds, much as Huxley imagined, through our rapidly growing understanding of the basic genetic cell designer material, desoxyribonucleic acid, or DNA. The molecular codes we now read incipiently will swiftly be mastered, and man will be able to predetermine as well as have advance notice of the next man's specifications.

A mechanical womb has actually been sufficiently perfected to keep a fetus alive for hours by forcing oxygen through its skin at 200 pounds of air pressure. Dr. Kermit E. Krantz, of the University of Kansas Medical Center, has built an ingenious device which hooks up to and simulates a real human placenta, supplying the fetus with food, oxygen, hormones, and antibodies, as well as carrying off wastes. A Dr. Petrucci in Italy is reputed to have mated a sperm and ovum artificially in his laboratory and kept the new life alive fifty-nine days; he has been accused of murder for terminating one of those experiments. Certainly our scientists don't intend to experiment forever on Rhesus monkeys. Dr. Charles Price, at a recent meeting of the American Chemical Society, formally proposed that test-tube life be adopted as a national objective.

While birth *control* measures already enjoy widespread approval, perhaps some of its detractors are more appreciative of the sad part the new *pill* will play in increasing man's control of life. *No* control of life, aloof from the God of life, can be practiced with impunity. The anti-ovulation hormone tends to amputate sex from procreation, as though a button could be pushed. It brings up the harder question: "In the last analysis, who prescribes for the pill user—scientific regulation, self, or God?" We must step reverently between the population explosion and a more insidious *Silent Spring*. The more mature moral issue raised is: Is sex without any responsibility or risk of children right for the unmarried? Despite the supposed need for a prescription, bootlegging of the pill already flourishes on campuses and even in high schools.

Dr. Hafez, whose research grants include one for $110,000 from the National Institutes of Health, "speculates that only ten or fifteen years hence, it could be possible for a housewife to walk into a new kind of commissary, look down a row of packets not unlike flower seed packages, and pick her baby by label. Each packet would contain a frozen one-day-old embryo, and the label would tell the shopper what color of hair and eyes to expect as well as probably size and I.Q. of the child" (ibid.). No doubt the back of such a packaged child will advertise Step II: microfilm library packages for the profession desired, plus chemicals for injected education.

How would you like to have your child receive an education from Oxford University in the same way we receive a series of penicillin injections? Our knowledge may someday be read as certain molecular structures. We have been learning geometry the hard way. Why not get a dose of it at the doctor's office?

If we are not careful, we may gradually squeeze the life out of existence, so that a boy's life will become a dead-run of inbuilt controls, predetermined from beginning to end. Parents could be sure he was safe, for he would respond like a record player to given situations. He would be tailor-made to fit the opening society had made ready for him. But how could he grow strong without strain? He would not be a person. The mysterious, unpredictable quality we refer to as "the human element" would be eliminated, and instead of a boy, we would have a heart, lung, and brain machine. Such a registered society of champions would have no more room for the treasure of a Tiny Tim than Dickens' Victorian London.

Life, liberty, and the free pursuit of happiness surely could be lost in the development of automation. Our adventures here upon the earth could be reduced to a groove of computation. Who would be the mother to such a man-made boy? The blank-faced creatures in Huxley's world think of "mother" as a dirty word indulged by their primitively crude forebears. Having been mass produced in an up-to-date Center, they like to sing as men would sing if they were decanted instead of born:

> For there ain't no bottle in all the world
> Like that dear little bottle of mine.

The noble sacrifice of a mother could be practically abolished by hiring a laboratory supermarket to deliver a tiny replica of her husband. Children suffer now from lack of personal contact; if they are hurt by oscillating affection, imagine their emasculation if they were deserted by cold mechanics to a mother of stainless steel in a Pavlovian clinic? What would life be, cheated of the luxury of a lap to sit on, appreciated about as much as a toy in a store?

Won't this manufactured man be dead? When someone is programed, is he not then reduced to some *thing?* He becomes slave and serf to the toymaker who wound him up. Will the little bits of babes (Carl Sandburg called babies "God's Kisses") become duplicate bottles of cut-and-dried man-made stereotypes? If so, the future holds a squalor the caveman never knew. Life will no longer be an art but a science of rigging the human machinery with stereophonic ears and electric eyes. The inhuman creatures will echo empty words like dolls who croak a taped assignment when a string is pulled. A biological factory may carbon, but without the touch of a more creative hand, there will be no more originals.

It could happen—if "science and technology would be used as though, like the Sabbath, they had been made . . . as though man were to be adapted and enslaved to them" (Huxley). Shall science pronounce sensuality "god"? What a great society it will be if inefficiency is the sin against the Holy Ghost. We might make men preveniently guaranteed to be mechanically moral; we might meet monthly to get our sin-immunity shots. We might perpetuate earth as a corporation too exclusive for God. Who cares? Technology can take over.

Who cries, "Ridiculous"? Who is playing God now to an American people who last year spent as much on gambling as on national defense? How long has it been since Sunday school assumed a fraction of the importance of vocabulary. If a child had to choose between taking home a straight-A report card or a religious experience, he would have little choice. Yes, of course, we want him to have God, etc., but in the meantime, night after night, we work exclusively on the new math. What about the aftermath? Who knows when the fatal line is crossed and human beings become the *means*, and the new math, or the whole world of science, becomes the *end* for which we live?

The usual space age forecast cannot locate many "homes" after about A.D. 2030. Homes are pretty precarious now. Cynics may have a case when they assume that homes will soon be swallowed by dormitories. Humanity is to become a promiscuous hive with interchangeable parts, and it will be highly unethical for people to go steady or be truly intimate. The tightening convention will eliminate friendships, and contacts will be hit and run—how can there be "progress" if there is permanence? In this "enlightened" realm, solitude will not be permissible, and no one will be able to comprehend the dreams and tears of *Romeo and Juliet*. Nothing will be worth dying for, let alone living for. In order for emotion not to get out of hand, it will never be indulged; it will be tranquilized out of existence. Sensuality, protected by the pill, will substitute for love.

This is where Huxley's soma comes in: "Christianity without tears, that's what soma is." When any grief or shame upsets us, we will stupify it promptly with pills. We will also, of course, singe our nerves and sear any recalcitrant conscience by going to the "Feelies," which will be like television with arms and legs, perfumes and electric shocks.

Our country is already doused in drugs. Fifty thousand junkies in New York City alone are spending all the time and money they can steal on narcotics to be "swinging high." They make *1984* old-fashioned. Catherine B. Hess, a member of New York City's Department of Health, describes the day the dope addict puts in:

"The addict wakes at 7:00 or 8:00 A.M. with jitters and unrest. His six hours are up since the last shot and a few withdrawal symptoms are starting. He immediately "skin pops" (takes a subcutaneous hypodermic injection). About noon, he hits the street touching base first with his fence to find out what needs to be stolen that day. In short order the material items are heisted and subsequently liquidated at the fence's quarters. The addict now has cold cash to begin his search for a pusher. If the supply is good a pusher can be found on any street corner in Harlem or Bedford-Stuyvesant. If the supply is short, hours of traveling may be needed, with every minute a panicky stressful situation in the fear that he may not find it soon enough to prevent withdrawal symptoms. After the "junk" is bought at $5 per bag (his needs are 4—5 per day), he searches for places and people to shoot-up with. Finally, in a dark, stinking, dirty "pad" the utopia of survival is experienced for a few miserable hours and then the process starts all over again. About two or three o'clock the following morning he finds some place to bed down for the rest of the night. Thus ends his exciting day!" (*Wooster Alumni Bulletin*, October 1965).

"The desire to take medicine," Sir William Osler said, "is perhaps the greatest feature which distinguishes man from the animals." And the majority of Americans are flirting with these tinier "goof balls," the sleeping pills, or more measured soporifics such as tranquilizers. Truck drivers stay awake on jags of amphetamine to collect more overtime pay; students pressed for time, or eager for kicks to fill their spiritual vacuum, do the same. No one damns the disciplined use of barbiturates, but the benders of glue-sniffing, or the wierd nightmares of LSD (which turned a pair of tennis shoes into a rabbit for one user), and the cavalier attitude toward chronic dependence on drugs—all of this represents the approaching anesthesia of mankind. Drugs are not free; they have side reactions, and generally sap vitality. Dr. André Sarran reminds us of the history of Mer 29: "This was an anticholesterol product that was launched on the market with an amplitude possible only to big business. . . . It was noticed that . . . after three or four years, Americans who had undergone preventative treatment in respect to cholesterol suffered from opacity of the eye-lens, loss of hair, and premature aging" (Paul Tournier, *Fatigue in Modern Society*). One woman was a nervous wreck because she couldn't get anything done. Her table was always piled high with ironing, and her desk with unanswered correspondence. She went on Miltown, and someone asked her how it worked. She said, "Well, I still don't get anything done, but now I don't care." If a drowsy driver "takes a psychotropic drug or stimulant, in a few minutes he feels full of euphoria and dynamism. He thinks he is the champion of the Indianapolis '500' and takes the curves on two wheels, passing cars that are passing other cars. The instinct for self-preservation is practically neutralized" (*ibid.*).

There is a place for modern medicine, but the immature can't use it without help. Unsupervised, or supervised by doctors, profit-motivated we take a pill instead of facing and solving a problem. Rather than expressing our grief at the graveside, we smother it with a "little something." Instead of bringing our life to order, we cheat on our sleep, batter our conscience into insensibility, and evade every moral crisis with medicine's cheap relief. Instead of doing something about our lives as though God were in the picture and we had to pay a price, we'll take something that will erase our distress. Don't control yourself—take an aspirin! We bury ethics in a barrel of barbiturates or, in extreme cases, we have the guilty area in our brain surgically removed. If we keep this up, life will no longer be a pilgrimage, ". . . that they should seek God, in the hope that they might feel after him and find him" (ACTS 17:27, RSV). It will become a pain-reducing exercise, a stultified Nirvana induced intravenously and not won on the nobler battleground of character.

Our morals must also meet the challenge of Technology Versus Age and Death. We must begin in gratitude for the modern abolition of much barbaric misery. We are all indebted to doctors and pharmaceutical research scientists far more than we like to admit; but the time has come when we must come to terms with what life is, how to act our age, and how and when we are to leave the physical life graciously. What must be the Christian attitude toward death in an age of longevity extended indefinitely, if not infinitely, as worn-out organs are replaced with spare parts? And who will you be if you walk around in your nineties with dacron arteries, donated glands, a cow's kidney, and maybe—with a transplant from a chamelon—a capacity to grow an amputated leg back on? Is death not an honorable thing sometimes? Must it always be regarded as one more pitiful failure at the hospital?

It has already become so commonplace to restore heart-beats and "resuscitate the dead," that we have begun to wonder if such restoration is always a favor. Professor

Robert C. W. Ettinger has written a book entitled *The Prospect of Immortality*, in which he recommends that bodies of the dead be frozen instead of buried or cremated. Ettinger proposes not looting the bodies for organs, but keeping them intact until future medical science can restore life. Would the souls come back? No doubt we would have to fight discrimination toward "restored" men, or these Rip Van Winkles might organize to gain equal rights with other job-hunters.

Ten cities in the United States presently enjoy branches of the Life Extension Society. "Recently a man in Springfield, Ohio, almost succeeded in having his wife's body frozen, but medical authorities withheld the needed cooperation" (*Life*, October 1, 1965) and now one has succeeded in California. Is not the war against death to be seasoned with Paul's "desire to depart, and to be with Christ" (Philippians 1:23, KJV)? Is Peter Pan the only one who can thrill to that assignment: "To die will be an awfully big adventure"?

The awful prospect in *Brave New World* was that nothing ever grew beyond teen-age in men, except their doctored memories. The faces of the dying were still fresh and unwithered, for "senility galloped so hard it had no time to age the cheeks—only the heart and brain." More and more men from our own generation die distracted—eyes glued to television, fears squelched by medical euphoria, wearing expressions of imbecile happiness.

Anything that interferes with the fullest development of each man, anything that does his thinking for him, or robs him of originality or creativity, is unethical. Technology changes, and men may keep the Commandments in a different way, but the chief end of man in A.D., 3020, as it was for Calvin, will be "to glorify God and enjoy Him forever." Jesus Christ has no quarrel with technology as such, nor is He prejudiced in favor of the scientific decor of a particular age. He is interested in something better than a better kidney or an improved refrigerator, in "a beauty too rich for use, for earth too dear." He came, not to take us away from all this, but so that we "might have life, and . . . have it more abundantly" (JOHN 10:10, KJV). Without God, the noble world of man could be reduced to some form of George Orwell's *Animal Farm*; but under Him, all life's chilling fiends could become good angels. We could rise to a golden age far superior than Edward Bellamy envisioned in *Looking Backwards* from A.D. 2000.

The meaning of life is beyond the mechanics of it. It is hidden in the total surrender of each man before the living God. A new epoch is beginning when more is required of us than body-repair and pain-control. One is no longer a Good Samaritan simply because he blandly sews up someone or keeps him alive. There is more to it than that. No one quite knows what is expected of him. But we know that all depends upon Him in whom we place our trust, and whether we can listen carefully in the darkness now, as Isaiah did: "And thine ears shall hear a word behind thee, saying, This is the way, walk ye in it, when ye turn to the right hand, and when ye turn to the left" (ISAIAH 30:21, KJV).

No one in his right mind wants to roll life back to the "good old days" of typhoid and inquisition. The followers of Jesus Christ look upon the future without fear, anticipating an unbelievably glorious event of which they are so sure they would not be shaken, ". . . though the earth be removed, and though the mountains be carried into the midst of the sea" (PSALM 46:2, KJV). Let come what will come, God's will is welcome.

# 14

# A More Excellent Way

"AND I WILL show you a still more excellent way" (I
CORINTHIANS 12:31, RSV). With that ringing sentence, a
Roman prisoner finished the spell-binding passage that
placed love on the throne of virtue forever. In all literature
Paul's lines have rarely, if ever, been surpassed. He sent
them to Corinth, but Corinth saved them for the rest of us,
and one day men from all over the world gathered together
and under the spell of the Holy Spirit, perceived that what
Paul said was surely the Word of God, and reverently
placed it among the sacred pages of Holy Writ. It is known
to us simply as the Thirteenth Chapter of First Corinthians.

"Though I speak with the tongues of men and of angels,
and have not charity [love], I am become as sounding brass,
or a tinkling cymbal" (I CORINTHIANS 13:2, KJV). Speech
judges today don't list *love* on their score cards. They miss
the whole point. Paul dismisses eloquence as noise if it lacks
love. Teachers go to the library to prepare their lectures,
preachers to their studies. Paul declares their work worthless
unless it comes from the heart. Correct greetings, campaign
promises, marriage proposals, compliments, apologies,
sermons, nice little thank-you notes say nothing, unless they
really say "I love you." A storm of words pours from the
lips and leaps from the presses and pounds on our window
and beats at our door. What is it? Paul got up to investigate,

and declared it was nothing but hot air—unless love made it.

"And though I have the gift of prophecy, . . . and all knowledge; and though I have all faith, so that I could remove mountains, but have not charity [love], I am nothing" (v. 2, KJV). If we knew what Russia might do next, and could see up the road ten years ahead and read how warm the war could get; if God would break down and tell us all His secrets—the date of Armageddon and Kingdom Come—endowing us with the wisdom of Solomon, what would this loot of information do for us? Nothing! Though we knew it all, but had not love's morning light, we would still be prisoners of the night. There is "a still more excellent way" without which, though we were as omniscient as Eternal God, it wouldn't mean a thing.

Though we were blessed by the Sinai faith of Moses; though we wiped out every obstacle in space, whipped every evil cell and fatal virus, abolished death with deep-freezers, and learned at feverish last how to conceive and stockpile our own men, yet had not charity, these erector-set triumphs would soon crumble and we ourselves would shrivel into monsters of success. Extending life renders a questionable service. As St. John said, ". . . we have passed out of death into life, because we love . . ." (1 JOHN 3:14, RSV).

"And though I bestow all my goods to feed the poor, and though I give my body to be burned, and have not charity [love], it profiteth me nothing" (1 CORINTHIANS 13:3, KJV). We can multiply our Christmas baskets for bare holiday cupboards; we can carefully sweep up all our crumbs for the sake of every starving Lazarus, make mountains of powdered milk, and dump the whole load of our surplus on barren shores—if offered without a little bit of love, we won't have gained a thing. We could shove our whole plateful across the global table, pull a St. Francis and sacrifice all our possessions in one grandstand play of philanthropy. It wouldn't work. It wouldn't work off our guilt complex, nor make us happy, nor gratify our insatiable desire to look good. It would not kill envy nor breed good will. It might murder self-respect. We could lay down our lives fighting for others' freedom, but men are starved for something more than bread and liberty. Until we supply that almost unknown quantity, nothing can change this hostile climate nor defrost the accumulated fears and prejudices that have drifted across the wrinkled face of our embittered earth. Until we first fall in love, we are profitless "do-gooders" with our wealth.

Christianity coined a new word for love: *agape*. It is not a romantic love, like *eros*, nor coldly platonic, like *philos*. It is too big a word to grasp at first. Paul pronounces it slowly for us. It is, he begins, ". . . patient and kind" (I CORIN-THIANS 13:4, RSV). This love does not get nervous, but knows how to sit still and wait its turn. It has all the time in the world, and when its time comes it is gentle and tender.

". . . love is not jealous or boastful . . ." (v. 4, RSV). This love is not cursed with possessiveness, as if its object were its property. It is not suspicious, for it is not contingent on another's constancy. It doesn't care how it looks. It does not make demands, swagger, nor show off. It has forgotten itself and forgets to sign its gifts. It is not loving for credit, but because it wants to, so is not resentful if not rewarded.

". . . it is not arrogant or rude" (v. 5, RSV). The Bible and not the book of etiquette is the authority on good manners. Paul could speak of manners with firsthand knowledge, for he had met the only "Perfect Gentleman." Only love eliminates the insolence between the lines. Only love can keep familiarity from becoming vulgar. When the bleeding woman tugged unseen at His hem, Christ did not shake her off; nor did He shove away the harlot who sacrificed her life's savings to wash His feet. And when they dragged the adulterous strumpet before Him so He could say, "Be stoned," He saved her with words that taught the world courtesy. All that King Arthur's knights knew of chivalry, they learned from Him. His "love," His apostle said, " . . . Doth not behave itself unseemly . . ." (v. 5, KJV).

"Love does not insist on its own way . . ." (v. 5, RSV). No one ever actually says he has to have his own way. We insist it is the way things have always been done, or that it is right; yet all our perfectly good reasons may be rationalizing what we want. Love does not have so exalted an opinion of its own point of view. It is wholesomely aware of its limits, and can easily appreciate someone else's side, be concerned about another's feelings, be confident that someone else could be just as intelligent. This love will not be forced to give in, but volunteers first. It is anxious to make sacrifices for peace, because, by standing in someone else's shoes, love finds it so much easier to believe another may be right. Love cannot help itself.

" . . . it is not irritable or resentful" (v. 5, RSV). Sour stomachs and sleepless nights cannot excuse our waspishness. It takes venom to snap and sting. Hate below bristles above with static; words become weapons and prickle with unkindness. But this love is in a good humor since things are going well with God. A Christian mirrors the sunniness in his Master. Love can get angry, but it saves the biting sarcasm for itself and unleashes its pent-up fury on pride, as Christ did. Love is very brave. It is said that "perfect love casts out fear" (1 JOHN 4:18, RSV). So love does not have the time nor the memory to carry chips or bear grudges; it is too busy believing the best and giving the benefit of the doubt. Love overlooks slights, and heals the unkindest cuts of all. If wronged, it leaves the punishment to God, but prays to Him to have mercy, as did the Man who hung on a cross. This love is digging an inexhaustible well of good will, with God's help.

". . . it does not rejoice at wrong, but rejoices in the right" (I CORINTHIANS 13:6, RSV). The malicious spirit is eager to know the worst about another; it savors juicy bits of scandal, vigilant in its search for more. It must believe all others are as bad as it is, and paints them so. Where it cannot prove the guilt, it imagines it; it leaves "not even Lancelot brave nor Galahad clean." Love steps over this and "rejoices in the right." This is the second mile, and a steep one it is. But to exult in another's happiness is a feat of magnanimity. To cheer for the victor takes something "still more excellent."

"Love bears all things . . . "(v. 7, RSV)—in sickness and in health, in the face of unfaithfulness.

> . . . Love is not love
> Which alters when it alteration finds,
> . . . .
> O, no! it is an ever-fixed mark,
> That looks on tempests and is never shaken.
> William Shakespeare, *Sonnet 116*

Nothing can stop it. There is no stronger steel. The world smashed Love against a Cross, and the dead weight of the whole world's sin fell on Him, but could not crush Him.

Love "believes all things . . ." (v. 7, RSV). It will not give up. It will never despair. God has given us creation "carte blanche." Christ trusts us completely. The prodigal's father was so sure his boy would be back that he never left the window, but watched with such unwearied confidence that years later he saw the boy coming while he was yet a great way off. Love can believe anything, even a miracle in the cold war next door.

Love "hopeth all things . . ." (v. 7, KJV). Love is a disciplined optimist, not afraid to look ahead, not unwilling to look for something better. It will at least go and check the tomb.

This love is forever. Love "never faileth: but whether there be prophecies, they shall fail; whether there be tongues, they shall cease; whether there be knowledge, it shall vanish away" (v. 8, KJV).

> The tumult and the shouting dies;
> The Captains and the Kings depart:
> Still stands Thine ancient sacrifice,
> An humble and a contrite heart.
> Rudyard Kipling, *Recessional*

"So faith, hope, love abide; these three; but the greatest of these is love" (v. 13, RSV).

# 15

# Prize and Punishment

"IN A CALIFORNIA market a young boy stood in front of the fruit counter stuffing grapes into his mouth as fast as he could. No parent was in sight and the inexperienced checker stood helplessly by. Suddenly a woman appeared, stared in horror at her son and shouted, "Johnny! Not so fast" (*Reader's Digest*, November, 1965).

Morals are being sacrificed in our sophisticated scrap for survival. Greedy eyes are glued to the pinnacle of the pyramid, not on the climb, for America's obsession is to have it made, hang the cost.

Our honor system can be stretched, if necessary, but our family and our teachers certainly would never tolerate our failure. Morals can become a casualty of the crash program of campus head-stuffing. Trophies are presented to winners, no one cares quite so deeply about how we play the game nor pays respect to the glory of honorable defeat. We damn the stupid rather than the dishonorable and prefer being intellectual to being true. The unforgivable sin is getting caught.

Modern man has almost persuaded himself that he can get away with sin. Many of our professors have swept God out of the way with wishful thinking, and many more have managed to dismiss the abominable idea that He gives damnation or glory according to what we do down here.

Accordingly, it isn't considered smart to believe in hell any more. "Good God wouldn't hurt a flea, let alone little ole me," so we fling His name around rather flippantly. "God's gone, or He's gone soft," some of us say. We excuse someone's misconduct thus: "It takes all kinds of people to make a world." We indulge instead of forgiving someone's mistakes with an "After all, we're only human." We have squeezed sin into our slang until the gangsters don't murder any more; they merely "take somebody for a ride." Adultery disappears into smooth talk: "They're enjoying a meaningful relationship." The stern proverb, "Spare the rod and spoil the child" was in *McGuffy's Reader*, remember? And if someone is a strict disciplinarian today, we dress him in grandfather's beard. This "easy come, easy go" philosophy has drifted into our concept of citizenship until a boy who doesn't like a law can burn his draft card. Unbridled behavior kicks constitutions and commandments up in anarchic air.

Arrogant unbelief may be as blind as blind obedience is bigoted. "Crime doesn't pay"—or does it? If it doesn't, we cannot cut corners on our income tax or levy a discriminatory poll tax without suffering for it sooner or later. That little fellow stuffing his cheeks with stolen fruit may temporarily get away with nothing more serious than a stomach ache, but sooner or later his bill for irresponsibility will come due. If his mother laughs it off, the poor lad must learn a harder way.

The Pardoner in his sermon (Chaucer's *Canterbury Tales*) offered a classic illustration to prove that "crime doesn't pay." Three thieves pulled a job and prepared to celebrate, and one went for refreshments. While he was gone, the other two got to thinking, as thieves will, how nice it would be if they could divide the loot into two piles instead of three; so they made arrangements to knock off the absentee. However, the same bright idea struck the third knave out there shopping for the provisions: he much preferred the whole haul for himself. So, during the festivities, the two knifed the third, then drank the poisoned wine he had prepared for them.

Seldom do men pay so neatly and promptly for their mischief; but they will pay absolutely. No one can get away with murder, nor with anything else. Usually immediate capture is the most merciful sentence of all, for the poor rascal who gives the police the slip lands in the drawn-out torture of the grind of years. The man who burned every incriminating clue behind him, and knows he's not a suspect, is haunted still by a more relentless uneasiness that will never leave him till he dies—and who's so sure it ends then? A wiser man will turn himself in rather than be hounded by that eternal conscience that ruins his rest and wrecks his nerves. The three thieves escaped mercifully compared to the desperate, otherwise decent men who once juggled figures or pulled a fast one, and who must take that recurring headache to bed with them every night, sleeping with the nightmares it gives them, and waking up in the morning to the reeking taste. A man may avoid the courts and keep out of the papers, but life itself adds on a morals charge of its own in the most mysterious and totally unexpected ways.

We noticed in Chapter Six how our morals can make or break our health, and that is only the beginning of a bad ending. George Buttrick told of a man with a guilty conscience who had taken a train to his country house:

"His family, eager to meet him, drove two or three stations down the line. They sent the trainman through the coaches calling his name: "Is Mr. Such-a-one on the train?" Instantly he feared that the police were after him. His sin had so clouded his judgment that he mistook his family for the police. It is no surprise that the scheming politician always blunders, or that the tyrant overreaches himself, or that any pride goes before a fall; sin blinds judgment" (*Christ and Man's Dilemma*).

"Be sure your sins will find you out" happens to be more than a cliché. Even the pettiest criminal pays for the tiniest infraction.

Morals are important to the man who believes he must answer ultimately for his actions. "G. K. Chesterton rightly contended that a landlady considering a lodger should not ask him first about his income. Her first inquiry should be about his doctrine of God and the universe . . . from that faith all conduct flows (George Buttrick, *op. cit.*). A man who knows he's under observation, and will be held responsible to a higher authority, is a better risk than the fellow who may be glib about God but really thinks nobody's minding the cosmic store. So the electric chair is, ideally, a deterrent to crime rather than a delicious revenge, just as the reminder of my father's razor strap kept me in line when not in use. The most permissive parent would sprain his son's arm to prevent him from running in front of a flying sportscar. As much as Russia may resent the threat of massive retaliation, no one doubts that it acts as the only restraint bullies understand. The social pressure to succeed placed upon youngsters today would make Puritans turn pale. The threat of demerits, demotions, detentions, and the loaded gun of expulsion or outright rejection hanging heavily over the head of every salesman and schoolboy is testimony to the persistent belief that the promise of punishment disciplines behavior. Anyone who has read this far recognizes the extensive Christian system of ethical checks and balances; yet man is less likely to flirt with evil if he knows he's on camera, skirting sudden death.

Morality is more than an academic question to be tossed

to the experts in theology; morality is mixed up with our meat and drink, and the morning mail. More important than its immediacy, our morality is a matter of life and death. According to the Bible, we are going to hell or heaven; we are justified by faith, not works, but we must remember that "faith without works is dead" (JAMES 2:26, KJV). The same Book that stresses the right spirit and pure motive is simultaneously preoccupied with the record of activity. Jesus' parables ring with our obligation to jump in and do the will of God, or else. The extremity of need screams for us to do good on earth for heaven's sake. Dives descended into hell to stay obviously because he didn't care what happened to Lazarus lying at his door. God, in one of the parables, called one man a fool for hoarding his surplus; and the drastic distinction between sheep and goats on judgment day depended on the record of whether men had fed the starving, clothed the freezing, comforted the sick, and visited the prisoner. A lawyer once queried Jesus: ". . . what good deed must I do to have eternal life?" and the Master testified: ". . . keep the commandments" (MATTHEW 19:16–17, RSV).

More persuasive than the threat of punishment is the prize promised to faithful men and true. Heaven may not be a legible incentive to pop-art cults, but eternal life is offered rather frequently in our New Covenant with Christ. We ought to appreciate how thoroughly the New Testament accentuates the "Crown of Glory that fadeth not away." ". . . lay up for yourselves treasures in heaven, where neither moth nor rust doth corrupt, and where thieves do not break through nor steal" (MATTHEW 6:20, KJV). Just as a man is slowly poisoned and embittered by the suspicion that death's lurking around the corner, so the bright prospect of permanent security is an incomparable stimulant: ". . . that your youth is renewed like the eagle's" (PSALM

103:5, RSV). Critics of Christianity may call our Easter confidence "poorly motivated nonsense," but the pertinent fact persists, as C. G. Jung declared in *Modern Man in Search of a Soul:* "All the patients who have come to me over thirty-five years of age fell sick because they lost their faith in God or in immortality."

The threat of extinction slings a long shadow down the road of life, devaluing the physical constitution far in advance. How happy is the man who actually believes that nothing can separate him from the love of God! If a man believes that the end of life is oblivion, it will blight his behavior long before. If he regards the end as fulfillment, it will lighten his load with blessing from the beginning.

The prize is no remote pie-in-the-sky proposal, but a "very present help." Our hope in heaven is not divorced from our happiness in this good life. What can compare with the delight of having nothing to hide? How delicious is forgiveness, to be freshly swept of bitterness! How precious is the tender assignment of peace, equipping one to trust! What pleasure can equal that of being able to lie down at night, composed by the Presence? The man who reaches for life as if it were a grab bag is robbed in the act. It *is* in giving that we receive. That line came hot from the experience of the One who reported directly from the front: ". . . seek ye first the kingdom of God, and his righteousness, and all these things shall be added unto you" (MATTHEW 6:33, KJV).

The long story of mankind has been about God's blessings on man's good behavior and the wrath of God on man's misbehavior. Adam is removed from Eden for eating the forbidden fruit. Cain is cursed for killing Abel. The great flood follows hard on the heels of the world's moral depravity. God knows when His nation, or anyone in it, breaks His laws, and God is just. All the mercy in the New Testament, so exaggerated at the present time, does not displace that justice. St. John himself, as Paul Tillich reminds us, ". . . is especially emphatic about the law of love, the disregard of which destroys the relation to God" (*Biblical Religion and the Search for Ultimate Reality*).

The ethos of the Bible bears down hardest on the burning issue before each one of us, which is in effect: *Shall we obey God or Baal?* Everything is at stake, depending on whether we shall decide for or against Christ.

Supremely, as St. John said, ". . . we have passed from death unto life, because we love . . ." (1 JOHN 3:14, KJV); but he astutely prefaced it with: "My little children, these things write I unto you, that ye sin not. . . . And hereby we do know that we know him, if we keep his commandments" (1 JOHN 2:1, 3, KJV). Lacking a sense of direction in love, we must necessarily lean on divine directions which define love for us. Moses said to his people, "Lay to heart all the words which I enjoin upon you this day, that you may command them to your children, that they may be careful to do all the words of this law. For it is no trifle for you, but it is your life" (DEUTERONOMY 32:46–47, RSV).

Now, when so many seem anxious to fling overboard the maps and laws long cherished by our fathers, and to steer by dead reckoning on some vague love, we wonder if those ancient manuscripts are not still shining from successful use and might be just as dear in directing us aright. Let us hang on tightly to senior ideals, for God never spoke lightly. As Richard Lovelace lined so beautifully to his beloved:

> I could not love thee, dear, so much,
> Lov'd I not honour more.

*To Lucasta, on Going to the Wars*

· 155 ·

Finally, we shall not forget that the love of honor is *inspired*. The One "Who for us men and our salvation came down from Heaven" came "not to drive us by moral imperatives" (*Life*, October 16, 1964). Rather, "I, if I be lifted up . . . ," He said, "will draw all men unto me" (JOHN 12:32, KJV).